MOTIVATING WRITING IN MIDDLE SCHOOL

Standards Consensus Series

National Council of Teachers of English
1111 W. Kenyon Road, Urbana, Illinois 61801-1096

Production Editor: Jamie Hutchinson

Series Cover Design and Interior Design: Joellen Bryant

NCTE Stock Number 52872-3050

Library of Congress Cataloging-in-Publication Data

Motivating writing in middle school.
     p.   cm. — (Standards consensus series)
NCTE Stock Number 52872-3050.
Includes bibliographical references.
ISBN 0-8141-5287-2
  1. English language—Composition and exercises—Study and teaching (Secondary)—United States. 2. Middle schools—United States. 3. Motivation in education—United States. 4. Experiential learning—United States. I. National Council of Teachers of English. II. Series.
LB1631.M68 1996
428'.0071'2—dc20
                                      95-49421
                                           CIP

CONTENTS

3. **Emphasis: Real-World Writing**

4. **Emphasis: Peer Editing, Self Editing, and Student-Teacher Interaction**

INTRODUCTION

RATIONALE FOR THE STANDARDS CONSENSUS SERIES

Much attention is given to matters that divide the teaching profession. But when NCTE collected dozens of standards statements, curriculum frameworks, and other key state curriculum documents in order to prepare *State of the States: A Report on English Language Arts Content Standards in Each State,* considerable agreement was evident in many areas of English language arts instruction. Similar consensus has been demonstrated in the development of the NCTE/IRA *Standards for the English Language Arts,* the core document that outlines national standards in our discipline.

A heartening fact has emerged from the standards movement, as varied as that movement has been: We are after all a community of teachers who draw upon shared instructional traditions in literature, composition, language, and related areas. Furthermore, in recent years the insight and invention of teachers and teacher educators have built upon those traditions in fascinating ways. The result is a rich body of practice-oriented material that parallels the mounting consensus in the profession.

NCTE has developed the Standards Consensus Series, then, in recognition of the existence of core beliefs about English language arts as revealed in innumerable standards-related documents and classroom ideas generated by teachers. The assumption underlying the series—and illustrated in it—is that good teachers have long been carrying out English language arts programs and classroom activities that exemplify sound implementation of the commonly held standards. The contents of each volume in the Standards Consensus Series were selected mainly from a database of classroom-practice materials. The database materials had been selected by teachers from a larger body of writings previously published by NCTE, mainly in the popular *NOTES Plus* journal.

Between the covers of this volume you will find some of the most exciting of the classroom experiences that deal with one major area of consensus in the profession—the teaching of writing in middle school. Below is a sampling of statements from various standards documents that testify to our common belief in the teaching and learning of various aspects of writing:

> *South Carolina*—Students use personal experience, the printed word, and information gained from observation as a basis for

constructing meaning. . . . Students use language for a variety of real purposes and audiences. (13, 15)

North Dakota—Students use knowledge and experience to write; identify a topic for a composition and determine its development; identify personal strengths and weaknesses in writing and seek feedback from others to improve writing. (31)

Arkansas—Students will use writing as a means of exploring thought and as a process involving prewriting activities, drafting, receiving feedback, revising, editing and postwriting activities, including evaluating, publishing and displaying. (1)

Massachusetts—Effective communicators . . . construct and convey meaning through the processes of reading, writing, speaking, listening, viewing and presenting. They understand reading, writing, speaking, listening, viewing, and presenting as communication processes. (39)

Kansas—Students write by generating, selecting, rethinking and reviewing ideas, resulting in effective communication for different occasions, audiences, and purposes. (13)

Michigan—All students will view themselves as authors and actors and . . . demonstrate their ability to use different voices in oral and written communication for various purposes. (13)

Alabama—Students will use critical, creative, and logical thinking when reading, writing, speaking, listening, and observing. (n.p.)

Vermont—[The student] expresses him/herself with power and purpose. (12)

Maryland—Writing is a means of self-discovery, of self-expression, and of clarifying what one believes, knows, or feels. . . . The learner: experiences the satisfaction of writing clearly, effectively, and honestly; chooses writing not only as a means of communicating with others but also as a means of learning and self-expression; recognizes the power and influence that conscious control of language in writing can give. (4)

Minnesota—Each learner will master writing to explain, describe, and express a point of view and feelings. (10)

These varied and powerful expressions of belief in the importance of writing point to the usefulness of this collection of materials on motivating writing in middle school as a key volume in the Standards Consensus Series. Of course, this is not to suggest that this book is of value only to those seeking to establish relationships between standards and instructional practice. Every high school teacher of English language arts will find a wealth of lively, academically well-grounded ideas in this volume. Even if there had been no "standards movement" as such, these materials would nonetheless present a profile of exemplary practice worthy of emulation in improving students' performance in English language arts.

A few comments about the nature of the materials and their organization are in order. Consistent with NCTE position statements and with the texts of many standards documents, most of the classroom practices included here do not isolate the motivation of student writing as if it were unrelated to the entire range of English language arts skills and topics. The materials in the Standards Consensus Series demonstrate amply that good teachers often do everything at once—asking students to reflect and talk about their personal and vicarious experiences, encouraging them to make notes about their readings and discussions in preparation for writing, encouraging non-threatening peer evaluation and self evaluation, and finding other ways to weave the language arts together in an integral learning experience.

A North Carolina goals document makes this point especially well: "Communication is an active process that brings together the communicator(s), the activity or task, and the situation that surrounds them. It is a constructive, dynamic process, not an isolated event or an assembly of a set of sub-skills. . . . Though listed separately, the [North Carolina] goals are not to be perceived as linear or isolated entities. The goals are interrelated aspects of the dynamic process of communication" (46). While the focus of this volume is mainly on motivating student writing, then, these classroom experiences typically exemplify the dynamics of real teaching.

ORGANIZATION OF THIS BOOK

Although the materials in this volume have previously been published in NCTE journals and books in recent years, this compilation is unique. No activity in this text is found in the senior high Standards Consensus Series text on writing, entitled *Teaching the Writing Process in High School*. Of course, you are invited to acquire that volume and seek out those materials that are adaptable to your classroom.

The materials in *Motivating Writing in Middle School* are grouped in useful ways that will be described below. However, neither the details of a particular classroom experience nor the arrangement of materials in this text is intended to be prescriptive. The day of know-all, tell-all books is past. Student populations differ; cookie-cutter activities simply don't work in every classroom environment. Most significant, teachers know their own students and they have sound intuitions about the kinds of ideas and materials that are and are not appropriate in their classrooms. From this solid collection of materials, teachers are invited to select, discard, amplify, adapt, and integrate ideas in light of the students they work with and know.

The topics of the sections in this volume—i.e., the emphases on artifacts; self exploration; real world writing; and peer editing, self editing, and revision—are not philosophically derived. Rather, they are useful ways of arranging some of the best teacher-selected materials from the NCTE database into a book that explores motivating middle school students to write. Other ways of compiling the materials are possible, but the emphases selected appeared to be most illuminating.

The organization and the contents of this book do, though, suggest an intriguing profile of how middle school teachers are able to channel the interests and energies of "middle-aged kids" into good writing. Most notable is the strong emphasis on *experiential learning* in Sections 1–3 in this volume. This is not to say that middle school teachers rely on personal experiences to the exclusion of literary and other vicarious experiences. Indeed, interspersed throughout the classroom activities in this volume you will find references to literary works that are excellent inspirations for student writing, e.g., O. Henry's "The Ransom of Red Chief," James Thurber's "The Secret Life of Walter Mitty," Judy Blume's *Fudge*, Beverly Cleary's *Ramona and Henry*, Daniel Keyes's *Flowers for Algernon*, and the poetry of Emily Dickinson, Robert Frost, Langston Hughes, Rudyard Kipling, Edna St. Vincent Millay, Shel Silverstein, Mae Swenson, and others. But such is not the main emphasis of this text. Another volume in the Standards Consensus Series focuses on teaching fiction in middle school.

The experiential activities gathered here are especially remarkable in their variety and ingenuity. Figure 1 depicts the range of experiential concerns in this book, and it serves as a visual schema for Sections 1–3.

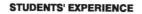

Figure 1.

In actual practice the various experiential components are not always separate. A self-exploration activity might also involve looking to the outside world; an activity that makes strong use of artifacts can involve sensory awareness; and so on.

In **Section 1—Emphasis: Using Artifacts** teachers show considerable invention in using concrete and familiar artifacts to motivate good writing. "Artifacts" here is used in a broad sense to include a variety of visuals (e.g., photographs, paintings, cartoons, and even ink blots), objects (e.g., hats, old phone books, dollar bills, masks, food, clothing, students' belongings), and audio recordings. Great resourcefulness is shown by teachers as they typically make use of inexpensive and readily available materials.

Moreover, the middle school student is cast in an active, meaning-making role in relation to artifacts. Students must create images implied in splotches of ink; execute brushstrokes that parallel haiku; infer narratives from names, pictures, or random objects; write poems from photos of school scenes; etc. Neither deadly formulaic writing nor vacuous gimmickry are evident in these middle school classrooms.

And again, activities in the "artifacts" section often spill over into other experiential areas. "Rorschach Revisited" is clearly a sensory exercise in visual acuity as well as a spur to imaginative writing. "Pressure" and "Looking Behind a Character's Mask" are strongly self-exploratory. "Writing under Protest" contains elements of both self exploration and critical thinking as students look inward toward their sense of justice and outward at real world social problems. The categories charted in Figure 1 as a convenience inevitably blur when one looks at the context of thoughtfully conducted classrooms.

Section 2: Emphasis—Self Exploration begins with three entries on sensory writing as students are asked to focus sharply on their experience of colors, odors, and multisensory observation. The section then moves toward helping students explore their inner worlds of memory, aspiration, value, and self esteem. With the ingenuity and insight that have become characteristic of sensitive middle school teaching of English language arts, introspective writings are stimulated in ways that are appealing, nonthreatening, and unintrusive. Sometimes, tie-ins with literature, as in "Daydreams: Our Secret Lives," "Finding a Special Place," and "Returning to Fairy Tales," provide the stimulus for self exploration. In entries such as "Two Truths and a Lie" and "Mind Reading as a Prewriting Tool," strong motivation is provided through nonthreatening interaction with classmates.

The entries in **Section 3: Emphasis—Real-World Writing** deal with *real audiences* for writing and with *gathering materials from and about the world outside the classroom.* The audience orientation in the opening activities shows middle school students writing for elementary school children, authors of books read in class, parents, and fellow students, both present and future.

Beginning with "Family Lore Writing Assignment," the focus is on students relating to worlds outside of the classroom. For example, students gather data for writing by interacting with family members and with workers on the job, or by discussing with each other their favorite hangouts or their feelings about social problems. Critical thinking comes to play strongly in the final three entries, "What's Hot and What's Not," "Making the Most of TV," and "A Prewriting Approach: Writing and Exploring Values."

Section 4—Emphasis: Peer Editing, Self Editing, and Student-Teacher Interaction brings the theme of motivating writing to important phases of the writing process. In essence, many of the motivational materials in Sections 1–3 are motivators for prewriting and drafting; and some (e.g., "Visual Contexts," "Collaborative Story Composition") deal with other aspects of process instruction. Peer editing, self editing, and student-teacher interaction merit special attention here because they involve the difficult task of helping middle school students to internalize criteria for good writing so that they can readily make use of those criteria, both individually and with others, as they consider revision. Many approaches are suggested in this section, from the self-check chart in "Evaluation Strategies" to students' metacognitive reports in "Writing about Writing" and "Don't Just Sit There, Talk to Me!" to various approaches to peer response and teacher-student interaction.

Figure 2 depicts some of the approaches to revision that are sampled in Section 4. Of course, many other approaches are possible. As with the various experiential sections, you are urged to consider the categories here in light of your own repertoire of motivational approaches.

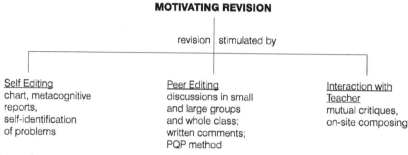

MOTIVATING REVISION

revision | stimulated by

Self Editing
chart, metacognitive reports, self-identification of problems

Peer Editing
discussions in small and large groups and whole class; written comments; PQP method

Interaction with Teacher
mutual critiques, on-site composing

Figure 2.

In a time of considerable pessimism and discord in education, it is encouraging to find major grounds for consensus in the teaching of the English language arts. In state and national standards statements that are being developed throughout the country, we find *common goals* for the teaching of our discipline. In the reported practices of the English language arts teaching community, we find *a formidable body of ideas about how to achieve those goals.* The Standards Consensus Series is both a recognition of cohesiveness and a tool for growth in the profession.

Finally, some acknowledgments are in order. First, kudos to the teachers and teacher educators who contributed their thoughtful practices to this collection, mostly via past issues of NCTE's *NOTES Plus.* The texts from that periodical are virtually unchanged, and the institutional affiliations of the teachers usually reflect their teaching assignments at the time of original publication. A few entries in this volume are from non–middle school or non–junior high levels (i.e., from high school teachers or teacher educators who work with middle school teachers), but all selections were judged to be appropriate for middle school use by the teachers who reviewed materials for the database.

Issues of *NOTES Plus* and other publications which were sources for this text have been regularly reviewed by chairs of the NCTE Secondary Section. These include the present chair, Joan Naomi Steiner, and former chairs Mildred Miller, Jackie Swensson, Faith Schullstrom, George B. Shea, Jr., Theodore Hipple, and Skip Nicholson. Staff coordinators and advisors for *NOTES Plus* have also been a key in this endeavor. The staff coordinator since 1985 has been Felice Kaufmann. The teachers who categorized the vast body of materials for inclusion in NCTE's general database of teaching practices are Carol Snyder and Jim Forman. This text was compiled by Charles Suhor, Deputy Executive Director.

REFERENCES

Alabama Department of Education. n.d. *Learning Goals and Performance Objectives.*

Arkansas Department of Education. 1993. *Arkansas English Language Arts Curriculum Framework.*

Kansas State Board of Education Outcomes Education Team. 1993. *Curricular Standards for Communication.* Attached draft of Wichita Public Schools curriculum standards.

Maryland State Department of Education (Maryland English Language Arts Task Force). n.d. *English Language Arts: A Maryland Curricular Framework.*

Massachusetts Department of Education. March 1995. *English Language Arts Curriculum Content Chapter: Constructing and Conveying Meaning.* Draft.

Michigan State Board of Education. September 1994. *Core Curriculum Content Standards and Benchmarks for Academic Content Standards for English Language Arts.* Draft.

Minnesota State Board of Education. 1988. *Model Learner Outcomes for Language Arts Education.*

North Dakota Department of Public Instruction. 1994. *English Language Arts Curriculum Frameworks: Standards and Benchmarks.*

South Carolina English Language Arts Curriculum Framework Writing Team. February 1995. *English Language Arts Framework.* Field review draft.

Vermont Arts and Humanities Commission, History and Social Sciences Commission, and Science, Math, and Technology Commission. July 1994. *Vermont's Common Core Framework for Curriculum and Assessment.* Draft.

1 | EMPHASIS: USING ARTIFACTS

PRECLASS WRITING ENHANCERS

I use a variety of preclass activities to complement my current goals for writing; such activities provide low-stress, enjoyable writing practice in important areas and put students in a positive frame of mind for the day's main pursuit. Each of the following warm-ups is intended to take just five minutes at the beginning of the class period; I use each one for one to three weeks.

HATS OFF TO WRITING

In this activity, students practice writing character studies and dialogues and think about point of view. You and your students will need to collect a variety of interesting hats ahead of time. As students enter the classroom, each one is asked to choose a hat and to imagine that he or she is the character who would normally wear that type of hat. Your current writing focus will determine which of the following assignments you will want to give students:

> Write a short, first-person narrative from the point of view of your character.
> Write a character study of your character. Include a physical description as well as personality traits.
> Write a short list of typical quotations from your character, or write a dialogue between your character and another person which reveals your character's personality.

AN EXERCISE WITH AN OBJECT

This activity gives students narrative and journalistic writing practice and requires some ingenuity. Collect a variety of small, unique objects and place them in a box or basket. Appropriate items might include a glove, a dog collar, a foreign coin, a candle, an envelope, a silk flower, a match book, and so on.

Either place an object on each student's desk before the class period begins or ask students to take an object from the basket as they enter the room. Choose one of the following assignments to give students:

> Imagine a situation or event that includes your object as an integral part. Write a one- or two-paragraph narrative or journal entry describing this situation or event.
>
> Write one brief, creative scene from a short story that would include your object. Write your scene as if it were an *excerpt*; don't worry about fully describing the characters or setting.
>
> Imagine that you are a newspaper reporter. Draft a short article for the front page in which your item plays an important role. Remember to use the five Ws: who, what, where, when, and why.

THE FRIENDLY ADVICE DEPARTMENT

In this activity, students practice problem solving and letter writing. Have ready a stack of legal-sized envelopes and 3-inch strips of blank paper. To begin, each student receives an envelope. On the front of the envelope, the student privately writes a question about an imaginary (or real) personal concern, signing a pen name like the ones used in advice columns. (In order for you to hand back the envelopes at the end of the activity without revealing any identities, you may want to assign students numbers to write on their envelopes in addition to their pen names.)

Suggest that students write questions which could have several possible answers. Sample student questions might be: "What can I do to get my parents to stop treating me like a baby?" "How do I let someone of the opposite sex know I like him or her without embarrassing myself?" "What should I do about a friend who talks about me behind my back?"

When students are ready, pick up the envelopes. Make sure the questions are in good taste and not too personal. The envelopes are then placed in a folder or basket near the door of the classroom.

Every day for the duration of the activity (two to three weeks), each student takes an envelope and a strip of paper upon entering the classroom. Students spend five minutes writing brief, friendly advice in response to the questions, sign their real names, and return the envelopes to the container. At the end of the time period, each student is allowed to read and to keep the peer advice given in response to his or her question.

Students really enjoy this activity. They give advice sincerely and look forward to reading suggestions concerning their "problems."

These preclass writing warm-ups are a good way to enhance a writing program. In addition, it boosts my own enthusiasm to see my students hurrying into class each day in anticipation of their warm-up activity.

Brenda Clark, Hildebrandt Intermediate School, Spring, Texas

RORSCHACH REVISITED

"Flowers for Algernon," by Daniel Keyes, continues to be one of the most popular short stories in my eighth-grade English classes. The popularization of its theme through recent movies such as *Rain Man* and *Awakenings* and television programs such as "Life Goes On" has increased students' appreciation of the problems of the learning disabled and the mentally challenged. Classroom discussion and reaction are revitalized each year as a result of these fresh perspectives provided by the media. Written response has been most productively stimulated, however, by something older than the 1959 story itself—the Rorschach test.

Our reading of the early progress reports that begin "Flowers for Algernon" leads us into a discussion of the Rorschach test and its importance in psychological testing. In the past I have invited professional psychometrists to visit our classroom to demonstrate and explain the actual Rorschach test. I have recently discovered, however, that a homemade version can be even more fun!

The students' first assignment in the unit is to create their own inkblots using ink, food coloring, or paint on a folded sheet of paper. The next day students trade their inkblots, and the excitement of the writing process begins! Lively brainstorming precedes the placement of a series of writing options on the blackboard. These options include such formats as poetry, top ten lists, deep thoughts, dialogues, and narratives. These are some of the ideas suggested by presenter Stephen Tchudi in a recent summer workshop.

I then take the necessary "risk" of sharing my own writing. I read a lengthy description of a Michigan lake, a description that developed from a cursory reading of an old newspaper article on drought. I share with much emotion a poem I have written grieving for my late brother, a poem inspired by a short story about a war. Once the students have seen the way many things can be used to stimulate a creative writing response, I encourage them to use their inkblots as their personal "prompts" to begin their journey into creativity.

After students have had the chance to reflect and then write their pieces, we completely rearrange the classroom for the group sharing that follows. A comfortable armchair is hauled in from the library, and student desks are positioned in a semicircle. Eager readers take their places in the armchair and share their writing while demonstrating their inkblots. Stories, scenarios, poems, impressions, and even songs are met with applause and appreciation.

Here are excerpts from two student writings, illustrating both a humorous and a serious approach to the assignment.

> *It reminds me of a butterfly*
> *Which looks so black that it is about to die*
> *It reminds me of Phil and Jen*
> *When they got caught kissing and their braces locked in . . .*
> *It reminds me of the time I read over this*
> *And saw more things but didn't make a list.*
> > —Reynolds B.

> *I see the world engulfed in two eyes,*
> *Two crying eyes,*
> *The tears gathered at the bottom do nothing*
> *But describe the pain and suffering,*
> *The hunger and starvation*
> *Of one without a home on a city street.*
> > —Shay B.

Conferring, editing, revising, and finally displaying the writings complete the activity.

The timeless appeal of "Flowers for Algernon" is enhanced by current popular culture, but the old Rorschach test prompts some of the most personal and enjoyable writing of the course.

Linda Wallman, Brookstone Middle School, Columbus, Georgia

ENGLISH, ART, AND HAIKU

Picture sixty students with *gahitsu* brushes poised. Picture sixty students counting syllables and finding synonyms in a thesaurus to enrich metaphors and other images.

Picture English teachers filling water containers and the art teacher checking spelling.

Result? A poem and a painting flowing from the same spirit to produce an aesthetic experience on rice paper.

How is this accomplished? It's easy. It's productive. But most of all, it's fun for teachers and students. Several days before the art teacher arrives at the English room with brushes, rice paper, etc., the students are busy learning and applying the techniques of haiku poetry writing. They learn that the Japanese spiritual poetry haiku was developed from an earlier form of Japanese spiritual verse called *tanka*. Basho (1644–1694) and his followers established haiku as a poetic form and brought it to its perfection during the seventeenth century.

This classical Japanese verse consists of seventeen syllables arranged in three lines containing five, seven, and five syllables.

> *See the red berries*
> *Fallen like little footprints*
> *On the garden snow*
> —Shiki, 1866–1902

Although concise, haiku presents insights into the nature of life—the reality and unity of spirit. The "image" of the poem transcends the direct experience of thought and language. Certain qualities are characteristic of haiku:

- The haiku must refer to an event or moment in time, not a generalization.
- Time is essential. And event is described as it happens now, not in the past. The poet gives a clear but brief view of the reality of a particular moment to bring about an almost transcendental

experience.

- The haiku should establish place. It is here and it is now, but in essence it can be almost everywhere.
- It should be a direct experience with nature and/or the seasons (season words are called *kigo* words). This experience evokes a mood—a fusion of seeing the scene and being part of it without intellectualizing the scene. All things have oneness with all other things.

To perfect haiku is to isolate a moment in time, to evoke a feeling by suggesting the overtones of the words. The Japanese believe that art is divine, that it presents the mysteries of nature in a profound way. By extending these insights from the mind to the hand to the fingers to the brush to the rice paper, this process of art—of creating—can be taken further.

The art teacher extends the experience through *suiboku,* the visual representation of haiku. Its purpose is to "display a noble soul" and to bring life to the *sumi,* the ink used in painting. The student must learn to "put all thoughts of self out of mind and become one with the spirit of the picture" (Ryukyu Saito). The mind must be quiet and the body relaxed but confident.

To instill confidence in students who may not have painted since elementary school, the art teacher begins with examples of *suiboku* accompanied by an explanation of materials using the Japanese words to set the mood:

gahitsu—brush used mainly for painting
sumi—soot from the smoke of burning oil, mixed with glue extracted from
    fish bones to make ink
tesuki—rice paper
katsuboku—giving life to the sumi

Next each student is given water, a *gahitsu,* a cake of *sumi* (in this case black cake tempera), and *tesuki* (newsprint). As the art teacher demonstrates the various brush strokes, students practice.

The following class meeting, students practice adapting strokes to create an illustration of the meaning of their haiku based on sketches they have done as homework. Stress is placed on leaving something to the imagination rather than producing a literal representation of the haiku. Most students are ready to duplicate their paintings on actual rice paper the next day. When this is done, the paper is folded at top and bottom, rubber-cemented together, and a dowel rod slipped through the folds. A black string completes the scroll effect and makes it ready for hanging.

Result? A finished product in which students learn they can paint as well as write. Because both haiku and *suiboku* are based on rigid disciplines, technical aspects are not a problem for even the insecure students. Instead, students are able to concentrate on the idea to be expressed and to learn that the mind and hand can work together to express emotional involvement.

Supplies:

> Black cake tempera—I for every 2 students
> Brushes—#7 watercolor for each student
> Container of water per student
> Paper towels
> Newsprint for practice, some cut to 6"x 12"
> Rice paper cut to 6" x 12" (allow 1" to fold over at top and bottom)
> Rubber cement (jar may be shared by many)
> Black string (approximately 18" per student)

Becky Duckro and Joan McKee, Bowling Green Junior and Senior High Schools, Ohio. This article originally appeared in English Journal, *November 1981.*

THE AUTOBIOGRAPHY OF A ONE-DOLLAR BILL
The Power of Observation

The students in my English class are not always enthused about writing, but the day we wrote the autobiography of a one-dollar bill, they were attentive from the beginning to the end of the assignment.

My preparation began the day before when I stopped at the bank on my way home from school and picked up twenty-three one-dollar bills. At the beginning of class the next day, I swooped dramatically around the room, slapping a dollar bill face up on each student's desk.

"I'm going to give you an open-book quiz on the dollar bill," I announced, instructing students to number their papers from one to twenty-five. I proceeded to ask the following questions:

1. What is the serial number on your dollar bill? Why do you think it appears twice?
2. What president is pictured on the bill?
3. In what year was your bill printed?
4. Who was the Treasurer of the United States at the time your bill was printed?
5. Who was the Secretary of the United States Treasury?
6. How many times does the word "one" or number "1" appear on your bill as designation of the bill's worth?
7. What is the name of the Federal Reserve Bank from which your bill originates?
8. What is the stated purpose of your dollar bill?
9. Look at the black circle with jagged edges on the front of your bill:

   What letter is inside the circle?
   What do you think the significance of this letter might be?

10. Look at the large circle on the left-hand side on the back of the dollar bill:

    What are the Latin words appearing above and below the pyramid?
    What do the words mean?
    What is the significance of the eye above the pyramid?
    What are the Roman numerals below the pyramid? What is the Arabic numeral equivalent? What is the significance of this number?

11. What is the significance of the eagle appearing in the circle on the right-hand side of the front of the dollar?
12. What phrase is written under the circle on the left-hand side and continued under the circle on the right?
13–25. Write down as many things as you can think of that you can purchase with a dollar or less.

Each student corrected his or her own paper as we discussed the answers to the questions. A lively discussion centered around the point of origin of each student's dollar bill (question #7). It was interesting to see how many Federal Reserve Banks were represented by the collection of bills in the classroom. The second question under #10 also intrigued the class, and I offered a reward to the first student to find the answer.

I then gave specific directions for writing the autobiography:

> You are this dollar bill. I want you to write your life's story in first person and narrate everything that has happened to you from conception to the present day. Be sure to include such details as your place of origin and how you came to be passed from owner to owner. Let us know your fate at the end of the story.

A quick look at the opening sentences of their rough drafts told me that the students had been very creative: "Hi! My name is Bill. Some of my closest friends just call me One"; "I was conceived in 1985, the son of my proud parents, Katherine Davalos Ortega and James A. Baker III."

I suggested that the students illustrate a particular aspect of their story and center their final draft around the illustration. This suggestion resulted in the discovery of a closet artist or two, whose abilities had gone unnoticed.

My students are often reluctant to read their written compositions aloud, but not this time. They not only produced some of their best writing of the year; they learned a lot about the dollar bill, too.

Jeanette Corkery, Jackson Alternative High School, Medford, Oregon

TALE OF AN UNUSUAL OBJECT

This prewriting technique helps my junior high students produce fresh, interesting stories later on.

I begin by holding up my "bag of tricks." In a red vinyl bag, I have collected as many unusual items as there are students in the class, including such items as a broken music box, a miniature microscope, a cheap gold chain strung with several charms, a rubber shark, and similar odds and ends. I take out one object and ask for reactions. Students usually describe the object's purpose or offer such comments as "That looks like the type of microscope you get with a chemistry set" or "They sell rubber sharks like that at the drug store."

I then tell my students that each of these objects has more to it than meets the eye. I concoct a tale about one of the objects, describing, for example, how the broken music box was the only clue to a murder mystery, or how the gold chain came to be found in a cache of stolen treasure. (I try to fabricate the tale on the spot, since an impromptu tale more accurately demonstrates the process students will use in their five- or ten-minute prewritings. Besides, students enjoy hearing their teacher develop a story out loud and on the spur of the moment.)

Once the mood catches on, I distribute the objects and give students five or ten minutes to sketch out their own imaginative tales in writing. I explain that I will redistribute the objects before each class period so that students begin new tales daily. After two weeks, each student has ten different possible plots from which to choose in developing a longer writing.

Cathy D'Entremont, Hildebrandt Intermediate School, Spring, Texas

| PRESSURE

There's one topic on which every junior high and high school student is an expert—pressure. Students know what it is to feel pressured, and respond positively to a writing assignment that allows them to express their thoughts and emotions on the subject.

Ask each student to bring in one object that represents pressure in his or her life. Objects that have appeared in my classroom have included a report card, a clock, and various musical instruments. On the next day, each student takes a turn at showing his or her object to the class and explaining in what way the object represents pressure to him or her.

Following the discussion, students generate a list of possible topics that relate to pressure, They may suggest such topics as kinds of pressures that affect teens, reactions to pressure, how I cope with pressure, or one particular type of pressure. After listing their topics on the board, I ask students to think of reasons for writing on the proposed topics. For example, they might write on "How I cope with pressure" to help other teens, or might explain "The effects of pressure" to help parents recognize if their children are under an unusual strain, or might describe one particular type of pressure to create public awareness of a problem. Thinking of reasons to write leads to a discussion of audience. I ask students to decide on the audience for their essays as soon as they have chosen a topic, and to keep that audience in mind as they write.

As students finish their first drafts, they may exchange papers and obtain responses and advice from other students. In addition to providing help in the composition process, this gives each writer a wider audience. Before students hand in their writings, I invite volunteers to read their essays orally. Often we select a Student Writer of the Week from these readings.

Karen A. Miller, Oldham County Middle School, Buckner, Kentucky

| WHAT'S IN A NAME?

These two exercises help students think about characterization and setting and are useful as prewriting activities prior to writing stories or as an introductory activity in a short story unit. You'll need an old phone book and several road maps.

Characterization
Give each student a page or two from an old phone book, preferably one from out of town. As students scan the columns, they should try to picture the people to whom the names belong. Sometimes the name of the street also triggers associations. When they run across a name that appeals to them, they write a short description of that person. Encourage students to make the character come alive by giving specific details about physical appearance, job, hobbies, friends, dreams and ambitions.

Setting

Cut up several old road maps into pieces approximately 3" x 5". Avoid sections that include names of familiar cities. Students then choose a name on the map that seems like a good place to develop as the setting for a story, going on to list details that help to create a setting—geographical features such as mountains, rivers, lakes, and forests; scenic or cultural attractions; industrial development.

Donna Weibel, Cascade Middle School, Longview, Washington

THE PAMPHLET: A SUCCESSFUL WRITING PROJECT

English teachers share two characteristics that make us a unique and amusing breed. We are print addicts, and we see the world as resource for our classrooms. As print addicts we can be seen reading the iced-tea container at football games, rereading the cereal box each morning, and taking one of every brochure at the motel in Disney World. And the world-as-resource lens has us collecting assorted paraphernalia because we just might be able to use it someday in our classrooms.

Somewhere in my travels (it was either an Interstate truck stop or a motor vehicle office), I picked up a pamphlet entitled "Sharing the Road with a Truck," published by the American Trucking Association. Over lunch I scanned its advice and warnings and somewhere between the fact that truckers fade left before they turn right and flashing lights were acknowledgments of my presence rather than flirtations, I realized that the pamphlet was interesting and well written. I knew I could use it somehow. I teach eighth grade English, so I saved it.

Because my students have varied abilities, personalities, and interests,

I often suggest writing projects rather than writing assignments. Even if the projects are small, I prefer them for three reasons. First, the idea of a project implies greater flexibility. Before beginning any project, there are three questions each student must answer.

> *Topic.* What am I going to write about?
> *Mode.* How am I going to write it?
> *Work arrangement.* Am I going to work by myself, with a partner, or in a group?

Since projects require attention to these weighty questions, they can eliminate those distasteful questions like "How long does it have to be?" and replace them with substantial questions like "I want to write a collection of poems about my friends. Where's that book of poems we read in the winter? Can I look it over?" and "Would a bar graph fit here?"

The same flexibility is available to the teacher. I can initiate a project by introducing a topic, such as shoplifting or friendships; a mode, such as stories, poems, or bulletin board displays; or a particular work group. Such freedom allows me to move my students through a range of topics, modes, and work strategies within a familiar arena—another writing project. The repetition of the format offers the students a security from which they can create and address new tasks.

Another reason writing projects seem particularly useful in junior high school is that they allow for individual differences. Given a topic, students can explore any part of it they are drawn to. If they are apprehensive, without ideas, or just in need of companionship, they can seek a partner or a work group. Most important, writing projects stimulate diverse writings so that students of varying abilities can work from their strengths but also feel free to experiment. As students learn quickly that it's difficult and pointless to compare a slide show/essay presentation with a poem, a short story, or a newspaper, their fears about comparative evaluation are diminished.

A third reason writing projects are successful is that they frequently begin with ideas collected outside the classroom. When students create travel packets, menus, or public polls, they replicate activities that are part of the real world. Our print-filled world supplies them with numerous models and the realization that people make money using language.

So I knew I could use "Sharing the Road with a Truck" some way. At first I thought I could use it to begin a letter-writing project. Students could write away for pamphlets about topics or places of interest. I became pamphlet and brochure conscious. I started noticing the hundreds that are available free and the dozens that cross my desk unsolicited each month. I began to notice layouts, designs, folds, paper. I began collecting pamphlets that advertised, informed, persuaded, and taught. They were expensive multi-color, multifold glossies and two-color, triple-folds with simple border trims. They were beautiful and boring, sophisticated and simple. My pamphlet folder bulged and the Pamphlet Project was born.

Essentially the project had three steps. I distributed copies of "Sharing the Road with a Truck" (generously donated by the American Trucking Association) and we discussed its contents. Students know a lot about truckers and discussion of the difficulties and dangers of trucking was lively and enriched by personal information.

The next day I displayed my pamphlet collection and we discussed the range of subjects and designs. We brainstormed brochure topics. Some mimicked the pamphlets we had: "Sharing Your Room with a Brother," "Eating in Iselin," and "How Not to Make Friends."

The third project day, students settled on a pamphlet topic and armed with supplies of paper of varying sizes and colors, with markers, crayons, compasses, rulers, magazines, scissors, and glue, we descended on the library for two days to gather information, if needed, and work on our projects.

I had thought "Sharing the Road with a Truck" was a good pamphlet, but "How to Cheat on Tests," "Tips for Babysitters," "Ten Ways to Annoy Your Older Sister," "Being a News Carrier," "Choosing a Dance School," and "Iselin: The Eating Experience" were better. Not only was the writing clear, focused, informative, and often witty, but the designs were colorful, attractive and clever. And the pamphlets were appropriately displayed on the bulletin boards because they were visually interesting and easily read.

One of the flattering features of writing projects is that colleagues steal them because they're so adaptable. A project is improved and expanded as it travels through the building and the folder becomes filled with donations and suggestions.

For the teacher, the Pamphlet Project is easy to introduce, enjoyable to work on, and incredibly pleasant to evaluate. For students, the project encourages them to choose a topic, design a format, and create a content that stimulates and pleases. It also provides an opportunity to demonstrate talents and knowledge from many content areas. The fact that they may be writing three to ten paragraphs about the topic somehow escapes them and they concentrate on putting together a publication similar to many already seen and read. Another plus is the tacit understanding that projects are meant to be shared, posted, read, displayed, or published. No one ever wrote a pamphlet to be read by only one person. Similarly, a controversial bulletin board is supposed to attract crowds, and radio plays are supposed to be taped and played.

Writing projects allow students and teachers to view writing in a new way each time another project is born. And since print addicts are always collecting for their classrooms, project possibilities are limitless.

Susan M. Skean, Iselin Junior High School, Fords, New Jersey. This article originally appeared in English Journal, *February 1982*

PICTURES TEACH STUDENTS WHEREVER THEY ARE

Multilevel classes offer special challenges for the teacher. With the burgeoning numbers of special-needs students in our language arts classes, including the many new immigrants and refugees who speak English as their second language, teachers need to find assignments that are open-ended enough for each student. With this assignment, all students can find success "where they are" as we address culture, punctuation, vocabulary, voice, and characterization in specific contexts.

1. Find a "Norman Rockwell"-type picture, i.e., any picture that is telling a story with people and a clear situation. *The Saturday Evening Post* is one source for this kind of picture.
2. Copy it for each student but have the original available for fine details.
3. Brainstorm on the board about the possible events and characters this picture illustrates. Place these words or phrases under headings like the examples that follow:

Characters	Setting	Situation	Vocabulary
Example 1			
elderly man	front stoops	summer	sidewalks
grown-up daughter	city street	afternoon	steps
father and mother			railings
next door			folding chairs
folding chairs			stroller
baby			ice cream cones
neighborhood			talking
teenagers			waving
ice cream vendor			knitting
			basketball
Example 2			
grandmother	dining table		
mother		Thanks-	turkey
son		giving	mashed potatoes
uncle		Graduation	
			throwing peas
			spoon
			bowl
			smile/frown
			angry/anger
			happy/happiness

This is especially important for nonnative speakers, who may need help with vocabulary and spelling. Of course, this step *may* be only oral for native speakers.

4. Ask students to write from one character's point of view. They may write about the character's feelings and thoughts, or tell the story that leads up to the picture. Encourage students not only to describe the picture but to invent an original background for the event illustrated.

    This is a good time to teach the literary terms of characterization, voice, and setting, as well as how to punctuate dialogue; many times these skills are needed within the students' stories.

5. The results of this task range from a restatement of the vocabulary from the brainstorming on the board to a detailed story with fleshed-out characterizations, depending upon the student and his

or her abilities; however, students see a finished product which reflects their efforts.

Gail Servoss, North High School, Eau Claire, Wisconsin

FROM OBJECT TO METAPHOR TO POEM

Of all the literary devices that we attempt to share with students, my favorite is the metaphor. For many students, this powerful device awakens a sense of the abstract and suggests new possibilities for creative expression.

After reading and discussing three or four poems that include metaphor (for example, Langston Hughes's "Dreams," Edna St. Vincent Millay's "Recuerdo," Ted Hughes's "The Lake," Emily Dickinson's "She Sweeps with Many-Colored Brooms") I ask students to flip through magazines, ads, newspapers, and so on for pictures that attract them. The pictures should include some nonhuman objects—animals, buildings, roads, trees, cliffs, and so on. The "attraction" may be a positive or a negative one (for instance, a student might be drawn to a picture that portrays a dark mood).

I ask students to think about what attracts them to the pictures they selected. After a few minutes, they jot down their impressions for each picture.

Next, students cut out three or four objects from their pictures. They close their eyes briefly and try to imagine themselves as one of their objects. To prompt ideas, I ask questions like "What does this object experience?" "What events or actions would it be involved in on a typical day?" "Where would this object typically be found?" Without talking, students open their eyes and write down their impressions next to the first list they made for the same object.

At this point, students write a poem in which they use their object as a metaphor. The "jot lists" of impressions can serve as a guide and give students a head start with descriptive words about their objects. I suggest that students think of their objects as representing them now, in the past, or in the future, but students have free rein to use their imaginations and envision their object in whatever ways are meaningful to them. They might want to talk *to* the object, as Emily Dickinson would, talk *about* it, as Langston Hughes would, write from the point of view of the object, or choose another means of conveying their message.

Sometimes I ask students to repeat this process with each picture they bring in (or cut out in class), and students choose the poem that they like the best to share with the class.

Students then paste their pictures to paper, pasting beneath them the poems they have created. I collect all of the pages and bind them into a book to display in the reading corner in my classroom.

Besides the deepening understanding of metaphor that results from this activity, the framework of pictures and jot lists provides a comfortable and low-key way to explore poetry writing.

Marti Singer, Georgia State University, Atlanta

COMIC STRIP PANACEA

Looking for a new idea for teaching writing skills? I have found comic strips from the daily newspaper to be the closest thing yet to a panacea. The short stories produced by students from this rather unlikely source are entertaining reading and take about two weeks to complete. This activity may be especially useful just before the holiday break, when thoughts are less likely to be strictly academic.

First, I write the creator of a particular comic strip for permission to photocopy and use in the classroom a particular panel from his or her comic strip. I like to use "Ponytail" because my eighth graders relate well to it.

After receiving permission, I blank out the dialogue on the comic strip with typewriter correction fluid and make copies for all students. Distributing these copies, I ask students to color the strip with markers, to study each character and setting carefully, and finally to write in appropriate dialogue. Besides being enjoyable, coloring the strip requires students to examine each part of every frame and gives them a chance to form their own interpretation of the action.

When students have colored their comic strips and written in dialogue, I collect the strips and set them aside for a few days. During this time I assign a story with good character sketches and dialogue; O. Henry's "The Ransom of Red Chief" is a good choice. After students have read the story, I explain the essentials of a good character sketch and hand back the students' comic strips with instructions to write short character sketches for each of the characters. I also ask students to devise and make notes on a setting for a story, based on the drawings in the comic strip and their character sketches.

Next, we discuss other elements of a short story: introduction, point of view, conflict, plot, climax, etc. With these elements in mind, students are asked to look at their comic strips and imagine the feelings of each character and what might have happened just *before* the scene shown in the comic strip. This information is to become part of the introduction to the student's story. At this point students should also decide on the point of view they want to express.

Students then imagine what happened *after* the scene in their comic strips—how each person might respond to the action and the dialogue shown and how each character's responses might in turn influence the other characters involved. Students jot this information down, too, and it becomes the basis for the plot and conclusion of their stories.

By this time, students have become thoroughly acquainted with their characters and are ready to finish developing their plots. To help them with this step, I ask them to decide upon the element of conflict that will be the basis for their stories. Naming the conflict and considering how it might be resolved is the final step before writing the first draft of their stories.

Now students are ready to weave information from their jottings into a short story involving the characters and action of their comic strips. During the drafting, editing, and rewriting process, I encourage students to consider all the short-story elements that we've discussed and to exchange and discuss their stories with one another. It's fascinating to read and hear twenty or more very different short stories based on the same comic strip.

Joyce Simmons, Gladewater Middle School, Gladewater, Texas

VISUAL CONTEXTS

In this activity students engage in a divergent thinking exercise, write brief descriptions in the genre of their choice, provide evaluations of each other's work, and revise their writing. The handout (see p. 24) can be used with students across a wide range of ability levels, but it provides an enjoyable, nonthreatening writing assignment for students who are usually reluctant to write.

Instructions

Tell students that the assignment gives them a chance to exercise their imaginations while writing descriptions in the forms they find most comfortable. Distribute the handout and go over the instructions. Discuss *context*, since the word has applications in other areas of English instruction. (You might briefly remind students how sentence context gives clues to the meaning of an unfamiliar word.) Emphasize that artwork is not the main point of the assignment. Rather, the drawing is a rough sketch of the student's idea; it provides a starting point for the description.

Drafting

After students have completed the two descriptions, remind them to enter a pseudonym or a four-digit number on the handout and on each description, recording the name or number for future reference. Collect each student's drawings and descriptions, and redistribute them. No one should receive his or her own set of materials.

Peer Critiques

Ask each student to write, on a separate sheet of paper, helpful comments about the descriptions he or she receives. This informal critique should tell which of the two descriptions the reviewer liked better and why. It should also include at least one suggestion for improving each description. Ask students to focus at this point on the *ideas* in the description rather than on punctuation, spelling, and other details, which will be handled later at the proofreading stage. Students should sign their critiques with the pseudonyms or numbers they chose earlier.

Editorial Board and Proofreading Groups

Ask for volunteers for (or assign individuals to) an Editorial Board and Proofreading Groups. The Editorial Board reads each description, considers the peer critiques, and writes further comments, taking care to offer praise and constructive criticism. The Board then selects the ten most interesting descriptions. The Proofreading Groups discuss mechanics, using blue pencils to suggest changes in punctuation, pronoun forms, capitalization, and the like. Allow these groups to work independently insofar as possible, but be ready to provide assistance if they get bogged down or disagree on a point that you might arbitrate.

Revision

All handouts, descriptions, and critiques are handed back to the original writers, who identify themselves by pseudonyms or numbers, and undertake revisions based on suggestions from the peer critiques, the Editorial Board, and the Proofreading Groups. Tell students that they may revise in accordance with their own ideas if they disagree with the suggestions. Invite them to ask your opinion on approaches to revision.

Audiences

Collect all revisions. The ten descriptions selected by the Editorial Board as most interesting can be read aloud by their authors and placed on the bulletin board. Additionally, you might select other descriptions that you feel are worthy of "honorable mention" to read aloud or post. An interesting extension of the audience for this activity is to ask students enrolled in art courses to illustrate the ten papers selected by the Editorial Board. This should be done only with the consent of the student authors, and in connection with author-artist conferences.

Charles Suhor and Robert C. Harvey, Urbana, Illinois

Visual Contexts

Each of the pictures below is incomplete. Complete the pictures by sketching in a fuller *context* for the event taking place. *You don't have to be an artist!* Draw in a simple, freehand style; use match-stick figures if you like. Then select *two* of the completed pictures and, on separate sheets of paper, write a brief description of what is happening in each picture. Your descriptions may be humorous or serious. They can be written as literal descriptions, as short stories, or as poems. Instead of writing your name on this handout and on your descriptions, use a pseudonym (made-up name) or a four-digit number. Make a note of your pseudonym or number so you won't forget it.

drawings by Robert C. Harvey

LOOKING BEHIND A CHARACTER'S MASK

I devised this assignment to encourage my students to look beyond the obvious. I wanted them to look past physical appearance and try to discover what is happening on the inside of a character. Also, I hoped the activity would help them experiment with new vocabulary terms in describing a character's personality.

The activity requires about eight to ten class days and the following supplies: paper plates, scissors, markers, crayons, a paper punch, and string.

Students begin by making masks that depict an imaginary character of their own creation. It can be any kind of character or personality they wish. Using crayons or markers, they draw a face on the plate and then cut the plate away from the mouth and eyes so that they can speak and see while wearing the mask. They punch a hole on each side of the plate near their ears and tie a long piece of string in each hole. Encourage them to find costumes to wear and props to carry with their masks, enhancing the physical appearance of their characters. They will have several days during which to assemble materials.

Students brainstorm a list of questions that will help them determine the personality of the characters they have created. Their list usually includes such questions as the following: What are you afraid of? If you had a million dollars, what would you do with it? Can you describe any personal habits? When student have come up with about ten or twelve questions, they fill out a personality profile handout for their character based on these questions. Having their masks before them might inspire creativity, but as students record personality characteristics, they begin to look behind the mask at their character's inner feelings. Personality dimensions emerge that might not be obvious from merely glancing at the mask.

Using the personality profile handouts, students write a first draft of a personality profile describing their character from the first person point of view. They read their profiles aloud to a response group and then use the group's suggestions in revising their profiles. I then ask students to underline all the descriptive words that they use in their first drafts, to consult their dictionaries and thesauruses, and to try to substitute new words in the revised profile. This final character profile will eventually be displayed on the bulletin board.

Students don their masks and costumes and read their profiles aloud to the entire class. I photograph each student with an instant camera and display the photograph with the written profile.

I found that after my students had developed their characters' personalities, they were much better at looking beyond the physical appearance of not only a fictional character, but also a historical figure and even their own friends. They also had fun trying out new descriptive words, and I was quite pleased when some of these new words began appearing in other writing assignments too.

Betsy Damon, Osseo, Wisconsin

DESCRIPTIVE FASHION SHOW

We're really going to model an outfit?!" exclaimed the disbelieving student. "You wouldn't do that to us, would you?" The classroom is not the usual location for a fashion show, but with a few twists I combined descriptive adjectives and fashion into a classroom activity.

My goal was to enhance students' descriptive writing by giving them some tools to work with and showing them that using adjectives can be fun, pleasant, nice, sweet, and even great.

First, we needed to focus on the students' vocabulary, their tool for writing a descriptive paper. Students brainstormed "dead" words, overused words whose funerals were long overdue. Eagerly jumping up and down—this comes naturally to sixth graders—students volunteered to kill their words of choice. Everyone had a word: *sweet, fun, nice, super, weird, great,*

They were not stumped for dead vocabulary.

But it's one thing to recognize words not to use and another to find a way to eliminate or minimize their use. So we buried the dead words. Each student chose a word to lay to rest and designed its tombstone, complete with epitaph. With gravemarkers hanging from the ceiling as a concrete and constant reminder of the dear departed vocabulary, students no longer had any excuse to use these words. Throughout the year, while working and conferencing in groups, I would hear students admonish one another, "You can't use that word; it's dead. Can't you think of a better word?"

After a period of mourning, the class prepared to replace the expired words with new vocabulary, a bank of words they could refer to when writing, revising, or editing. I gave out colored strips of construction paper and asked each student to think of the adjective which best described him or her. As they all sat with blank stares, one student raised his hand and remarked, "But there are so many adjectives, how can I choose?" I smiled and responded, "Exactly. With so many from which to choose, your writing should come alive if you take time to think about the right word for the job."

Off they went to the dictionary, exchanging whispers and deciding to survey friends and family members for the "perfect" word. I made some interesting and insightful discoveries as they revealed themselves with their perfect words illustrated on their strips of construction paper. Each student hung his or her personal statement on the wall in the room, and this served as our vocabulary bank for writing. The room became a testimonial to dead and living words.

With all the words floating in and around the room, we needed some direct input onto paper. This is where the fashion show came in and students had the chance to show what they had learned about lively, descriptive words.

I asked students to select an outfit, write a complete description of it, and model the outfit for the class. Some students were apprehensive at the idea of parading around the room in front of their peers, until I explained that they had complete artistic freedom in their choice of outfit. From fashionable to silly, evening gown to paper bag, anything was acceptable as long as it was accompanied by an imaginative, detailed description.

I sent students on a search-and-destroy mission, a form of prewriting, to brainstorm an outfit and make notes on sensory details: texture (How does it feel? How does corduroy feel different from silk?); smell (What associations does this smell have for you? Does it remind you of your grandmother's perfume?); sound (What sound does your outfit make as you move? How does a full skirt sound different from jeans?); and look (style, color, the way the light hits the material, etc.).

For my part, I brought out my box of 64 crayons with the pencil sharpener in the back and shared my memories of wonder at the many colors inside the box. *Cornflower blue, lemon yellow,* and *violet* began to surface in student conversation and print.

Finally, after much preening at the mirror, we were ready to model our ensembles. (Teachers should feel free to participate in this activity as well!) A narrator read our descriptions as we pranced up and down our "runway." The elevator music softly playing in the background set the mood as the narrator assaulted us with fashion dos and don'ts. In my class, students have modeled—and described—lampshades, snowmobile suits, alien loungewear, and Grandmother's Victorian lace dress with antique jewelry. At the end of the class period, we talked about what we liked best in each outfit and description. Students posed for photos and later received one as a reminder of their day on the runway.

Nancie Atwell quotes Mark Twain at the beginning of Chapter 6 in her book *In the Middle:* "Don't say the old lady screamed. Bring her on and let her scream." On the day of our descriptive fashion show, we screamed, laughed, cried, and learned.

Lynn Fucci, Katherine Stinson Middle School, San Antonio, Texas

CLASSROOM CHEF

Although the students in my alternative English class range in ability level from third to twelfth grade, they have one thing in common: their mutual aversion to writing. But the day I fried an egg in class, I didn't hear one complaint about the writing assignment.

Looking like part of Julia Child's laboratory, my desk became my kitchen counter, complete with electric frying pan, utensils, and ingredients. (Be sure to find out in advance whether there are restrictions on the use of electrical appliances in class.) Less conspicuous, but as important, were the words I had written on the blackboard:

First
Then
Next
After
Finally

As the students settled into their places, I kept my instructions simple: "Today I am going to fry an egg, and I want you to take careful notes on everything I do." For the next ten minutes there was perfect silence as willing pencils recorded every step. When I finished frying the egg, I ceremoniously scooped it onto a plate and offered it to the bravest-looking volunteer.

I then asked the students to work their notes into paragraphs about what they had observed. I started them out by writing a beginning sentence on the board: "Our teacher, Jeanette Corkery, fried an egg in class today." Directing student attention to the board, I told them it would be easier to organize their thoughts if they used the connectives listed there.

For the first time I can remember, there was not one complaint as the students began to write. As they finished their compositions, I quickly made corrections and requested revisions. The next day, students were able to sample each other's writing when I read the compositions aloud. It was interesting for all of us to hear how much variety there was, given so structured an assignment; the ending sentences were particularly amusing.

The most rewarding moment of this lesson came the following Monday morning. One of my heretofore most reluctant writers came in before school and plopped a neatly written paper on my desk. "Here," he said proudly. "Read this." What he had given me was a well-organized account of a baby shower his neighbors had given his mother over the weekend. He had carefully chronicled the sequence of events by using the very transition words I had put on the board.

Jeanette Corkery, Jackson Alternative High School, Medford, Oregon

CLICK:
POETS AT WORK
IN THE MIDDLE SCHOOL

"I hate poetry!"
"We did that boring stuff last year, we copied poems!"
"I can't write that old junk—I'm not a poet!"
"I can't read or understand poetry; how can I write it?"

Immediately I felt the daggers hitting me as my students proceeded to tell me that they could not write poetry. But I was determined that eighth-grade students could learn how to write and enjoy poetry. Calming the classroom to get their attention, I asked why they were turned off to poetry and opened the class to discussion.

I learned that the students felt they did not have any experiences to draw on that would enable them to write poetry. They live in a small town and feel there is nothing to write about.

Class ended with an assignment for the students to survey their surroundings and to look for things to write about. The next day, when the students returned to class, they had nothing to share about writing poetry.

Well, this created a monster inside of me. I was determined to show them that they could write, that they had experiences and feelings to write about, and that they had poetry in the making in their hometown.

The next day, I took my camera to school and started shooting slide film of people, places, and things: pep rallies, football games, flags flying, boats sailing on the bay, the train station, Sylvan beach, Boys' Harbor, churches, schools, mansions, shacks, city hall, fire stations, new cars, chemical plants, and, most of all, the students engaged in different activities.

I had the slides developed, took them to class the next week, and said, "Okay class, today is the beginning of your poetry writing career." Slides flashed across the screen while music played in the background The students watched the slides and started whispering and laughing. I asked them to tell me what they saw in the pictures. As I flashed a picture of a sailboat sailing in at sunset, they shouted words such as: sails flying, water hitting, catching the wind, blue sail boat, red sky, white sails, blue sails, fun, soaring, waves crashing. While they were brainstorming with words, I wrote them on the board. I then told them these are words that poets use.

The next slide was a picture of a pep rally, and I told the students to use their five senses to come up with as many words as they could that described the picture. They came up with many words, including these: cheers, orange and white, fight songs, football players, friends, band playing, students rocking, stomping feet, clapping hands, competition yells.

I eased the class into writing a poem about the pep rally by asking for nouns, verbs and prepositions. They composed this poem:

Pep Rally

Orange and white
Pom Poms
People yelling
In the stands
Rocking to the music
All
Fired up!

Each day the students looked at a new slide and in groups of four brainstormed appropriate words. They then wrote simple poems until they got the feel of poetry. I was also reading from the following poets: Carl Sandburg, Robert Frost, Shel Silverstein, Langston Hughes, May Swenson, and Jack Prelutsky. Carl Sandburg's "Chicago" inspired the students to write poems about their hometown. Jack Prelutsky's collection of poems about Thanksgiving and Halloween gave the students ideas for their poems, as did the other poets. Discussing these poets and their unique techniques of writing, I pointed out examples of poetic devices—similes, metaphors, alliteration, onomatopoeia—and challenged them to find examples of these devices. When they found them, we shared them in class, and little by little the students began using poetic devices in their poems.

Some of the poems that my students wrote follow:

Thanksgiving Day Is Near

The holidays
The holidays
The days are filled with cheer.
With shorter days

And longer nights
Thanksgiving Day
Is near.

A morning chill,
And the red leaves
Are turning brown
With fireplace smells
And colored lights hung
All over town
Thanksgiving Day
Is near.

Big football games
With Aggies and
The Longhorns
A parade downtown
And Santa Claus
A fancy float adorns
Thanksgiving Day
Is near.

And then we go
To Grandma's house
With ones we hold
So dear
With Roast Turkey
and Pumpkin Pie
Thanksgiving Day
Is here!
　　—Eric

I Am a Blackman

Black is back
Black by demand
Black is beautiful
Black words from a Blackman.

A Blackman is strong
A Blackman is proud

A Blackman gets hype
He never gets loud.

A Blackman hates teachers
They get on his nerves
A Blackman likes girls
And all their great curves.

A Blackman has knowledge
A Blackman has power
A Blackman lives forever
And stands out like a tower.

A Blackman was beaten
A Blackman was shunned.
A Blackman was looked down on
By all the ignorant ones.

In school they teach us
How to read and write
But they don't teach us about
South Africa and their fight.

One day Africa will rise
The ignorant will fall
Black and White will live together
There will be love and peace for all.

In the immortal words
Of my hero Doctor King
Let freedom ring
Let freedom ring.

Too Black
Too Strong
Too Proud
These are the words
Of a Blackman
    —Darrin

One day I took a cut-out of the shoe of a local professional basketball player to class and had each group write a poem on the shoe. The poem contained words heard on a basketball court. The students then made an outline of one of their feet and wrote a poem about themselves on the tracing.

They wrote their poems on their own, and they realized that they did have a great deal to say about friends, pets, family, heartbreaks, music, and many other things..

Nancie Atwell (1987, *In The Middle*, Portsmouth, NH: Heinemann) says that

> when my students use writing as a way to capture their feelings, trying to give shape to their inner experiences, poetry is the mode to which they most often turn. (26)

I gave the slide camera to my students, and they recorded their world. They wrote poems about everything in their small part of the world in the shadow of the San Jacinto Monument, the Astrodome, Houston skyscrapers, and NASA—a world where people go to work as ships sail into port from around the world, while gas jets burn in refineries, and teenagers walk hand in hand. This is their world, an island almost unto itself.

Eighth-grade students are in a constant state of flux—one day they are in love; the next day they despise the one they "loved." They are changing constantly, and they do have the need to release their emotions, so let them write poetry. They do have the expertise to do it. Their emotions are merely actors waiting to be captured on film.

Action! Camera!

Eighth-grade students are making poems
as they pass through life.
Eighth graders are poetry in motion.
　　　Click
　　　　Click, Click
　　　Snap, Snap
　　　　Flash ! ! !
Poe, Frost, Lawrence
　　Recording words
　　　Into
　　　Thought

　　　A
　　　Poem
　　　!

Marjorie E. Connell, La Porte Independent School District. This article originally appeared in English Journal, *November 1990.*

🌺 🌺 🌺

WRITING UNDER PROTEST

It isn't fair!" How many times do you hear your middle-level students issue this cry? They continually rail against family, home, school, and life in general. Turning this cry into an instructive and exciting writing experience can be accomplished through the use of protest-song lyrics as poetry.

An entire week can be spent discovering the power of words and music to activate social change.

Day One

Read with the class any poem that has been used as lyrics for a protest song. I use the poem "After the Buffalo's Gone" by Buffy Sainte-Marie. After students have read the poem, play a recording of the lyrics in song form. Through hearing this poetry as music, students are better able to feel the emotional impact of the words.

Play examples of other protest songs. Be sure to have copies of the lyrics available so that the students can see the written forms. "Blowin' in the Wind," "Sounds of Silence," and "Brick in the Wall" are good examples. After students have had an opportunity to experience the variety of musical styles, they can perhaps share current protest-song titles with the entire class. Encourage students to find examples and bring them to class the next day.

Day Two

Brainstorm with the entire class any issues students feel are unfair. Stress that these may be personal, local, or global in nature.

Discuss how important it is to match the tone of music to the issue being protested. Review the previous day's songs (and any new ones students have suggested) to enable students to listen for volume, speed, major and minor sounds, and so on. The music teacher is an excellent resource for this lesson. He or she may be thrilled to be invited into a classroom to share musical information with students.

Encourage students to think of one or two issues that they would like to write about. Offer the following format:

The problem:
Why is it unfair?
Examples of situations that illustrate this problem:
How can this problem be addressed?

Day Three

Group students in threes. Have each student share his or her protest ideas with the others in that group. Encourage questioning and elaboration so that all members of the group have clear understandings of the issues being protested.

Ask each group to select the issue that it feels can most easily be converted into lyric form. Remind students that their writing needs to conform to specific rhyme and rhythm patterns.

By the end of this class period, each group should have selected an issue to write about, and a melody. The room will be awash with humming, singing, and excited wordplay as classmates begin to compose their protest songs.

Day Four

This entire class period can be spent creating lyrics. The teacher should be circulating to help any groups stuck with unwieldy rhyme or rhythm problems. Encourage the groups to sing their songs aloud so they can hear the impact of their lyrics. This is a good proofreading check for the rhyme and rhythm patterns as well.

Prepare students for their performances on day five. Ask each group to have a legible copy of its song ready to hand in the next day after the performance.

Day Five

Tape the groups' performances. Also collect a copy of each song when the students finish singing. These can be bound into a "protest songbook."

After each group has finished singing, allow a few moments for discussion. Seek meaningful comments from the students by asking such questions as how the song addressed the issue, if the tune chosen was appropriate, if correct rhyme and rhythm patterns were used, and so on.

Conclude the class period by handing out "Grammy Awards" to each group. Categories for these awards could include *Appropriate Musical Selection, Meaningful Lyrics, Use of Words to Fit the Rhyme and Rhythm Pattern, Unusual Song, Cooperative Group,* and *Singing Ability.*

By the end of this unit, students will have a better appreciation for the power of songwriters in society. As they struggle to create their own protest songs, they will come to understand that songwriting is a skill as well as an art.

Who knows? You may have inspired a budding songwriter!

Judith E. Foust, Menomonie Junior High School, Menomonie, Wisconsin

ACTIVITIES TO ENCOURAGE WRITING FLUENCY

These short, simple activities involve students in writing painlessly about what they've heard, seen, and experienced. They may be best used not as whole-class activities but to stimulate fluency for a student or students who have trouble keeping the "flow" going. The results of some of these activities might later be used as the basis for full-blown stories, essays, or other writings.

I have picked up a couple of these ideas from other teachers or from workshops over the years, and adapted them to my use. Special thanks must go to my friend and colleague, Karleen Good, who shared several of the original ideas with me.

Quick Read and Write
Read part of an interesting story to students for five minutes. At the end of five minutes, ask students to spend five minutes writing about what they heard. Then have them count the number of words they wrote. This exercise

is repeated daily, continuing until the story is finished. As the activity progresses, students tend to feel more comfortable writing and to write more in the space of five minutes.

As a variation on this activity, students may read to themselves, listen to a cassette tape or record, or watch a movie before writing.

Story from Photo

Show students an interesting photo or picture. You can show the same large photo to the whole class, or give each student a separate photo to look at. Ask students to write for five minutes about the photo. Then students take a word count and share stories about their photos.

Guided Image Writing

Give students the basic outline of a story and ask them to fill it in with details. For instance, students might add scenery, add animals, or describe the appearance of a storm. They might also add dialogue between animals or humans.

This type of guided image writing can also be used in other subjects, such as history or geography. Students might take a trip through another era or another country, describing what they see and encounter. Lead them to each place, and their knowledge and imagination will supply the details and the actions.

Draw and Write

The basic idea is to have students draw some kind of picture and then write about it. One of my favorites is to have students cut a paper circle, square, diamond, or other shape, from one to several inches across. The shape is then glued or pasted to a piece of construction paper and the class brainstorms ways in which the design could be used in a picture. Students then draw pictures, each one using the shape of the cutout and its position on the page as an important element in the drawing.

The drawings are then described in writing and shared with the class. This activity works especially well with younger students and with students reluctant to participate.

Word Description

Pick a noun that lends itself to description. Ask students to get the image of that item in their heads and then to write a description of the item. Give them five minutes to write. Ask them to take a word count at the end of the five minutes. To help students gain a sense of flow when they write, repeat this exercise often, encouraging them to increase their speed just a little each time they write.

Memories of Home

Ask students to recall the first house, apartment, trailer, or other dwelling in which they remember living. They are to sketch a quick floor plan of the living space, choose a favorite spot or room, and recall a pleasant incident that occurred there. Students then write a short description of the incident.

Larry Newman, Akers School, Lemoore, California

2 | EMPHASIS: SELF EXPLORATION

WRITING WITH
THE RAINBOW

My students and I were focusing on descriptive writing, attempting to add specifics to personal narratives. The goal was to put the reader *into* the events in the writing. But so far, the typical description I had read didn't get much beyond the usual bland adjectives—"big," "red," "green." The windows opposite my desk lured me beyond stacks of papers piled before me. There I encountered all the glory of nature's fall diversity—flaming orange, burnt umber, burnished gold. The season's multicolored delights coaxed an idea to take form.

The next day, instead of spending the hours indoors, I suggested that the class take a walk. I encouraged students to focus on the infinite variety of color around them, collecting a few leaves, berries, or twigs from those that had fallen already. Conversation along the way was lively, as students discussed the names of plants and the broad range of shades of color possible in leaves found under the same oak tree. (In another season of the year, or in a situation where a walk is not practical, this idea can be adapted by asking students to bring in small items with interesting colors from their homes or neighborhoods. As long as students find hues and shades that challenge their descriptive powers, this color-naming activity will be just as effective.)

Back in the classroom, students took their collected items—from tiny feathers to three-foot long tree branches—to their small groups. Each group's task was to select two favorites and create names from the *colors* of the chosen items. The goal was to achieve a color name so exact that an audience could visualize the precise shade of the leaf or twig selected. Animated discussion resulted. Boxes of crayons emerged as sources of ideas. One student held several crayons alongside a leaf of similar hue and checked the manufacturer's label for name ideas. Others resorted to brainstorming lists of all the color names they could recall from art class and then chose the most specific designation for their group's perfect feather. Still other groups suggested comparison after comparison until they found the most apt simile for the shade of an acorn or a pebble.

Once choices were final, groups lettered their created labels onto colored sentence strips and mounted both objects and labels around the room. Results ranged from poetic to ridiculous—tree frog green, bark brown, gaseous orange. Interest was high as groups congratulated themselves and each other on creativity and accuracy.

The following day began with a brief time for evaluating our efforts. Students selected what they thought to be three particularly interesting and apt color names, recording those in their writing logs along with some statement about why those titles appealed to them. Sometimes two different names for similarly colored items were both judged accurate; either name brought the exact color to mind. In those cases we discovered that readers were still likely to favor one name over another because of the sound of the words being spoken or because of pleasant associations with a particular label. "Firefly yellow" was not only more accurate but also more pleasant to hear and think about than "ooze green."

Students were quick to note, however, that not all writing calls for pleasant associations and that some of our accurate labels, though producing negative responses, could be quite effective in different contexts designed to provoke fear, anger, or repulsion.

As students were invited to consider how useful our collage of color names would be in writing their own personal narratives, they drew another conclusion. Natural colors, at least in the fall, tend to be clustered in a certain range of the spectrum. We were missing purples and blues and pinks almost entirely. What resulted was a spontaneous search in pockets, binders, and purses for items in the missing hues. Names for these shades were crafted, mounted, evaluated, and discussed.

A few days later, when those personal narratives began to pile up on my cluttered desk top, I was rewarded with rainbows of accurate, mood-capturing descriptions. *This writing had come to life!*

Carolyn Matteson, Calhoun Middle School, Denton, Texas

TRANSFERRING IMAGES INTO WRITING

"Fish sticks again?"
"Remember that stink bomb in sixth grade?"
"Coach Myers always smelled so good!"

Transferring images from one's experience into one's writing is a major step in writing development; however, images that activate the sense of smell are often omitted, despite their potential for adding the vital connection between writing and reality. The sense of smell is our most nostalgic sense. Compared with the other senses, odors are messages that last.

To encourage students to make this connection in their writing, it is necessary to demonstrate its validity, especially since middle school students often require proof for everything! The following activity provides a tactical learning experience which is the basis for the writing workshop. As Lucy McCormick Calkins says in *The Art of Teaching Writing*, "It is the content of real life, for the workshop begins with what each student thinks, feels, and experiences, and with the human urge to articulate and understand experience."

The activity begins when I place a recycled lunch box labeled "Caution, Imagery Enclosed" in a conspicuous location. I draw attention to the box only by asking the students to "Beware." Of course this is almost too much for them to bear for an entire week.

When the time arrives, I ask the students to close their eyes and imagine various scenarios (e.g., a hospital, a mall, Grandma's house). After they have "warped" to each scene, I ask them to take a deep breath to make sure they have arrived. I then ask volunteers to identify what they smell. We list the "smells" on the board. During this time, I find it effective to peek in the imagery box several times to further their curiosity.

After brainstorming a generous list, I disclose the contents of the box. It contains twenty baby food jars filled with scents or what I like to refer to as "imagery evokers." Using cotton balls to capture various scents has proven to be practical and less hazardous, particularly considering the tendencies of middle school students. I use the following:

alcohol	cough syrup	crayons	nail polish
cinnamon	soap	leather	baby lotion
wet dirt	deodorant	cologne	Play-Doh
peanut butter	menthol	vanilla	tar
hay	onion	bleach	lemon

We begin with an oral discussion using the cinnamon scent. After allowing each student to smell the scent, I ask the students to share whatever picture or memory the cinnamon inspires, reminding them that "the smell" may not necessarily play an integral part in their stories. The students become eager to share, and I allow several impromptu stories.

Anticipation is at its peak when I announce that we will be sampling nineteen other "imagery evokers." Distributing handouts for students to record each scent and related thought, I emphasize that they should write down the *first* thought that comes to mind. The jars are numbered and responses are written by the corresponding numbers. If the scent has no significance, I ask students to continue but to record what they think they are smelling. Because some students are over concerned with correctness, I also tell them that there are no right or wrong answers. In addition, it is helpful to start half of the jars on one side of the room and half on the other side. Since this is one of my favorite activities, I find a vacant desk and join in the fun. The students tend to get silly with this activity, so it is very important to preface the activity with very specific jar-handling instructions.

When we have all finished smelling, we complete an oral exercise using the cinnamon scent. For example:

> Cinnamon always reminds me of my grandmother when I was little because she baked the best cinnamon rolls I've ever tasted making me feel warm, special, and sad all at the same time. I wish she were still here.

Next, I have the students draw stars next to two of their favorite "imagery evokers" and complete the same exercise we completed orally. This activity doesn't produce finished products; instead, it's a device to help the students put their thoughts in perspective. From this point on, a myriad of possibilities exists. The activity can be easily adapted to student as well as teacher needs. It can serve as prewriting for descriptive writing in the expository and poetic forms. I have found myself in tears after reading a poem about a parent's funeral in which the smell of death was remembered after smelling a perfume. The perfume became flowers at the funeral home. Another student was reminded of dousing his toy soldiers with alcohol and setting them on fire when he was six. I took advantage of the situation and encouraged him to write from a six-year-old's point of view. The seed for point-of-view writing had been planted. The connections made between scents and reality never cease to amaze me.

Kipling, in his poem "Lichtenburg," wrote that the pungency of rain-soaked acacia meant home, and Proust said that the aroma of lime-flower tea and madeleines launched his monumental *Remembrance of Things Past* (Terrance Monmaney, "Are We Led by the Nose?" *Discover*, September 1987). Perhaps this activity will be the inspiration needed by our students to awaken a commonly untapped resource, the sense of smell, in the writing classroom to make the ultimate connection between reality and writing.

Terry Floyd, E. M. Pease Middle School, San Antonio, Texas

MY TWO-FOOT WORLD

This writing assignment is designed to encourage students to expand their descriptive vocabulary, use their senses to explore and describe their world, and write an essay in an organized, unified manner. An added benefit is that students seem to develop a greater appreciation for the things in nature.

This assignment would be applicable for many grade levels; I used it for seventh- and eighth-grade students' transition from paragraph writing to the writing of their first essay. It can also be adapted to paragraph writing or poetry writing, or used as a springboard to short story writing.

The steps are as follows:

Day One
As a warm-up to writing, ask students to suggest words that they use to describe things that they see, touch, smell, and hear. As students brainstorm words, make a list on the chalkboard, grouping words by the sense involved. In addition to the common descriptive words that are suggested, such as

"pretty," "soft," "flowery," encourage students to think of more unusual descriptive words for sights, sounds, smells, and textures. Some examples might be "mottled," "barbed," "pungent," and so on. This prewriting step will smooth the way for more imaginative descriptive writing the next day.

Day Two

Take the class outside and ask them to spread out in an area free from distractions, where they can isolate themselves. Tell them that they are to pretend that their world consists solely of the area in the two feet of land and space around them. In several paragraphs, students are to describe their "two-foot world" using the senses of sight, touch, smell, and hearing.

I tell students that their paper might include elements such as these: an introductory paragraph that includes the central idea—for example, "My two-foot world tantalizes my senses," descriptions of sights, descriptions of sounds, descriptions of textures and feelings (this could be external, internal, or both), and a conclusion that restates the central idea and brings the paper to a satisfactory close.

I stress that students are to try to apply the steps that we learned previously, where they moved from prewriting (clustering ideas), to writing a rough draft, editing, and "publishing." The editing and rewriting may be done as homework.

Days Three and Four

My method for publishing is to ask students to present their finished papers to the class. Students in the audience listen and write notes to critique each paper. After each paper is read, volunteers are asked to share some of their comments. In this way students have the benefit of reading their own writing, of hearing their peers' comments, and of formulating critical evaluations of their peers' writing.

Barbara Eubanks, Rainbow Middle School, Gadsden, Alabama

DAYDREAMS: OUR SECRET LIVES

Given my love for daydreaming, it should be no surprise that I like teaching "The Secret Life of Walter Mitty." I introduce the story by asking for a definition of a daydream. Students are eager to brainstorm what daydreams are, when they happen, and why they are so delightful, and I encourage the outlandish and the bizarre. After all, as one student recently remarked during this discussion, "Anything can happen in a daydream!"

Then we settle into several specific scenarios for some prewriting before both our reading of and our writing about the story. This year I challenged my sixth-grade students to imagine what would be the best experience in the next six years of their schooling. Numerous possibilities were shouted out: scoring the winning goal in the most important soccer game; receiving a standing ovation for a lead performance in the middle school play; hopping off the bus one afternoon to find a shining Lamborghini as a graduation present. After sharing ideas, students chose one and wrote about it, developing it through dialogue and description, all the while telling each other, "Wait until you read this!"

Before students became too attached to that daydream, I asked them to go beyond six years: "Imagine what you'll be doing twenty years from now," I exhorted. In a split second, my sixth graders had transformed themselves into scientists on the verge of creating computers to allow for time travel; contestants in the National Outdoor Typing Championship; and winners of the most lucrative of all lotteries. One student became a divorce lawyer on his way to court to argue the divorce of two of his peers in the class!

During the next class we read "The Secret Life of Walter Mitty." Thanks to the prewriting, my sixth-grade students didn't stumble too much on Thurber's sentence structure and vocabulary. Our earlier discussion enabled them to understand Mitty's associative daydreaming, and they were primed from their own writing to appreciate his continual metamorphosis into hero. After reading the story, we listed each of Mitty's dreams, contemplated Thurber's theme, and described the stylistic specifics of each dream sequence.

Now we were ready to create our own "secret life" stories based on the prewriting. Our model was the original, and we reread passages from Thurber to come up with ideas. We brainstormed possible opening sequences: being sent out of the classroom on an errand; dozing off during a discussion; putting a basketball into a locker before the start of class. Then students chose a daydream, some opting for one from the prewriting, others creating something completely new. All that remained was returning from the daydream to reality.

Several students volunteered to read their completed stories to the class. We targeted three areas for discussion: how well the author moved from reality to daydream; how well the daydream was developed; and how well the author returned from the daydream to the original situation. Making a smooth, logical connection between reality and dream proved the most elusive, but authors received valuable suggestions from classmates. My favorite suggestion was one directed to the student who daydreamed that he was an off-duty policeman making a drug bust of two notorious villains. The suggestion was that rather than simply dodging the bullets flying at him, the author catch the bullets in his teeth and spit them back at an even higher velocity. (The author decided instead that he would use his "superior running skills" to evade the speeding bullets.)

After our group discussion, we broke into smaller peer response groups. Through their reading and writing, students had developed a fine ear for the style of a "secret life" story, and their suggestions for revision were specific and imaginative. Almost all second drafts were more humorous and more thoroughly developed, and showed that students were learning to appreciate the subtleties of style.

We are still sharing these "secret life" stories, reading and discussing three or four each class period. Perhaps my most rewarding moment came when I heard the student who had once remarked, "This is a boring story," praise "The Secret Life of Walter Mitty" to a student in a different sixth-grade class and advise him to read it.

Margaret Hopkins, The Park School, Brooklandville, Maryland

THE REWARDS OF THE WANTED POSTER

When writing about themselves, my students are quick to list their problems and shortcomings, often overlooking their positive qualities. In order to help my students see all sides of themselves and to focus on what they like about themselves, I use a prewriting exercise called "The Wanted Poster."

At the beginning of this activity, I give each student a Wanted Poster form which looks roughly like the real thing. The form asks for *name, date of birth, a photo or caricature, physical description, caution,* and *reward.* Students could conceivably design their own, but authenticity is part of the appeal. One difference is that students may choose which of their physical attributes they feel comfortable sharing: height, weight, eye color, hair color, skin color, mannerisms, etc. I offer to take polaroid "mug shots," or students may bring their own snapshots from home or draw caricatures.

Under the heading "Caution," students list short phrases that describe problem areas. For example, a student might include *sarcastic sense of humor, short temper, selfish, disorganized,* or *puts things off until it's too late.*

The real focus of the activity is the "Reward" offered. Unlike the reward section of a real wanted poster, ours is reserved for a list of positive personal characteristics—a list that details how others will be "rewarded" by knowing this person. Students first spend a few minutes thinking about what they like about themselves. If students work in pairs, partners can exchange ideas on one another's best qualities. Then students make their lists, which may include phrases like "a good sense of humor," "loyal to his/her friends," "honest," and so on.

My students often have difficulties with the "Reward" section; they are in the habit of minimizing the good things they do. When students have trouble identifying their positive characteristics, I ask them to try listing people in their daily lives, to think of particular ways in which they help those people, and then to go on to list the positive characteristics involved in their actions.

The poster is not complete until the "Reward" section is at least as long as the "Caution" section. It can be a real eye-opener for students when they discover that their good qualities outweigh their less desirable ones and that they might be "wanted" for those qualities.

Mark S. Meisner, Eau Claire, Wisconsin

FINDING A
SPECIAL PLACE

Each of us has a place that is special. We call it our own and feel more comfortable there than anywhere else. In this place, we can be whomever we want and can dream all there is to dream.

I use this idea of a special place as a creative writing activity that also stimulates students to use their reading, speaking, and listening skills. Although I use this activity with fourth graders, it could be effective at many grade levels. It might be particularly beneficial in motivating reluctant learners to write and revise in a collaborative setting.

To begin, I read aloud *Andrew Henry's Meadow* by Doris Burn (Coward, 1965) to my class. The discussion that follows leads into a semantic mapping session of "What is a special place?" We depend on all our senses to create a list of as many ideas as possible for a special place.

Once the board is filled with the characteristics of a special place, the students' job is to think of various places that they feel are special to them. This activity is a silent one, and I give my students think time before they begin writing. When this time is up, I ask students to write eight of these places on their papers.

Students meet with partners and share their lists. They take turns reading off the places on their lists and also justifying why they chose those particular eight places.

Still working with their partners and discussing their choices, students narrow their choices first to three places and then to one place. This is their special place, and from this point on the partners share all that they can see, hear, feel, taste, and smell while at this special place. I have found that while one partner is speaking, the other needs to be involved in active listening, so I ask the listener to write down what he or she remembers as soon as the speaker is finished. This list can serve as a prompt for the writer to use in preparing the first draft of a paper about this special place.

Students begin their first drafts with freewriting. I want them to get the ideas in their heads onto the paper. Spelling, grammar, and sentence structure are not to be thought about at this stage.

Upon completion of the freewriting, students meet in their response groups. Papers are read aloud, and the group's job is to make suggestions to each writer for revision. I ask the students to pay close attention to how the writers use their different senses to describe their special places.

Students are given time to make revisions. They take the group's recommendations and add to or delete from their papers accordingly. Then students meet again in their response groups, and again the group discusses the paper and makes further suggestions for revision. Students make a final copy of their stories, either writing them by hand or using a word processor or typewriter. The finished papers are assembled into "My Special Place" books, which can then be shared with family and friends and displayed in the classroom.

Lynn Gamroth, River Heights Elementary School, Menomonie, Wisconsin

POSSESSION PARAGRAPH

One writing assignment that is often used successfully to motivate students is a request for several pages of unrestricted stream-of-consciousness-style prose on any topic that comes to mind. But providing free rein is not the only effective way to interest students in writing. A structured assignment like the following challenges students' resourcefulness and thus stimulates creative writing. I've had great success with this writing assignment that emphasizes descriptive detail. It produces papers with fascinating and varied content that virtually call out for sharing. The assignment I give is outlined below and has three major parts: general requirements, sample paragraph, and prewriting plan.

Requirements

Describe as accurately and specifically as you can your most valued possession, but do *not* mention what it is anywhere in your paper. In addition, your writing must meet these requirements:

1. Length: one fully developed paragraph with no fewer than six specific details describing your possession. You may write two paragraphs and double the number of details.
2. Your description must contain one comparison; for example, "a color like the whiteness of new-fallen snow."

Sample Paragraph

I think you'll guess my most valued possession before you finish the paragraph below. When you think you've got the idea, go on to the prewriting exercise that follows.

> Burnt orange, like an autumn sunset, it carries me over river, stream, and pond. Fifteen feet of solid construction, yet it glides smooth and silent, almost effortlessly guided by my strength and will. It is modern plastic in construction, yet to be in it reminds me of its birch bark forebears. Durable as technology can make it, yet it brings me back to the pristine beauty of raw nature. Like a beast of burden it carries me, my dog, a tent, sleeping bag, food and fishing gear, carries all to escape from the hustle and bustle of the mundane world. All this, yet I can carry it upon my shoulders when the need arises!

Prewriting

Close your eyes and bring to mind your most valued possession. Look at it in your imagination; walk around it in your mind to see it from all angles; climb up on something and look down on it from above. Now go on to answer in writing the two sets of questions below. Include the answers to the questions with your finished paragraph. If you have difficulty answering the questions, come back to the mind's eye step above and begin again.

Concrete Details
1. What color is your most valued possession?
2. What size is it?
3. How is it shaped?
4. How does it work?
5. What is its use (function)?
6. What does it smell (taste) like?
7. How does it feel to the touch?
8. Does it make any sound? What kind?
9. How did you get it?
10. How long have you had it?

Comparisons
1. If your most valued possession were an animal, what would it be? Why?
2. If it were a fruit or vegetable, what would it be? Why?
3. What season does it remind you of? Why?
4. How do you react when you have it near?
5. How do you react when you don't have it around?
6. Would it be enjoyed most by a young person, a middle-aged person, or an old person? Why?
7. What object in nature does it most remind you of?
8. What object in your house does it most remind you of?
9. Does it make you think of any person you know? Why?
10. What emotion best fits it?

Michael Dolcemascolo, North Syracuse Junior High School, North Syracuse, New York

MIND READING AS A PREWRITING TOOL

Becoming a mind reader only sounds mysterious and magical. I have found that the following prediction activity encourages the critical thinking skills of my students, improves their writing development, and promotes audience awareness.

Here are the instructions that I give to my students:

1. Think about four experiences in your life that you remember in detail, and list them on a sheet of paper.
2. Circle the one experience that is the most memorable.
3. On the front side of a sheet of paper, write content questions that you, the writer, will want to answer as you write about this experience.
4. On the bottom of the front side of the paper, write questions that you, the writer, think the reader will want answered in your story about the experience. (The questions should be different from your list of questions in Step 3.)
5. Turn your paper over, and in the upper left-hand corner of the paper, write the topic of the experience that you, the writer, have chosen.
6. Pair up with another student and exchange papers. Do not read the writer's questions from Step 3.
7. Write a list of content questions that you, the reader, will want answered about the topic chosen by the writer. Return the paper to the writer.
8. Compare the content questions listed by you, the writer, with those suggested by the reader. Were you a mind reader? Did you anticipate your reader's questions?
9. Share with the class the types of questions (both specific and general) that you did not anticipate that the reader would ask.

10. Write a first draft of your paper, using the questions generated by you and the reader.

This prewriting activity helps students generate content questions about their topics and anticipates questions that a reader might have. It promotes different levels of questioning and different levels of thinking. And the lists of questions help students as they revise their first drafts. Perhaps there's magic involved after all.

Jim Newkirk, Western Heights Middle School, Hagerstown, Maryland

TWO TRUTHS AND A LIE

Two Truths and a Lie is a storytelling game that we adapted for classroom use and have found very successful, particularly when we've used it as a beginning-of-the-year activity. Each participant tells three stories, only two of which can be true. Questions follow the stories and—when everyone has finished—participants guess the "lie."

For classroom use we begin by instructing students to generate vignettes of truths and lies over a broad range of topics. Typically, these include general categories, such as the following:

First memories
Strongest memory of childhood
"Believe it or not" tales of grade school
Stories of feats and accidents
Something I did when I was alone

Students have a prewriting period in which they can discuss possible topics, then ten minutes of quiet for each to write a first draft of a "truth." A small break provides time to pause or extend a draft; ten more minutes provide starter time for the lie, the fictional account.

Ultimately, each student has ten vignettes, half of which are truths. The student chooses two truths and one lie from these selections and polishes them for detail, development, and mechanics. The student labels the final written vignettes *A, B,* and *C.* Numbers may be substituted for student names to ensure privacy.

All the vignettes are taped to the wall of the classroom at shoulder height. Students read every selection as they walk around the room, recording their guesses of "truth" or "lie" on a worksheet they each carry. At the completion of this process, each author informs the class which of his or her selections are true and which is fictional. The students keep score of their worksheet guesses, and results are compared. Students can decide ahead of time to award points either for fooling others or for not being fooled.

The game has the advantage of being both a writing and an interpretive activity. Because students sketch more vignettes than they will eventually use, the structure of the assignment encourages a rapid generation of ideas in a criticism-free context. This is reinforced by the time limits, which work in freewriting fashion to accelerate drafting.

Moreover, because they are trying to fool their classmates, students select their vignettes and edit them with this audience in mind. Finally, the work of each student is published.

When guessing begins, the nature of the game shifts from composition to interpretation. Separating fiction from nonfiction points up distinctions between them, while the scoring process provides each author the opportunity to speak to his or her selections. We've learned to take our time with this step, allowing particularly good guessers to describe how they found the lie and encouraging discussion of how a particular writer was able to fool us.

Finally, one can't play Two Truths and a Lie without broaching a critical inquiry into the nature of fiction and nonfiction. Is fiction lying? Can one use it to tell the truth? Conversely, can nonfiction be used to lie? While the use of such questions depends on the age and grade level of the students, it is an accolade to the game that even the youngest of participants will raise them.

Steven VanderStaay and Mary Metzger, Iowa City, Iowa

RETURNING TO FAIRY TALES

Fairy tales and folk tales aren't just for children anymore. They offer adults and young adults a means to recapture some of the delights of childhood, and also offer students out-of-the-ordinary material for a study of some of the aspects of literature.

Fairy tales, folk tales, and other stories that fall into this genre are the basis of much of the literature of our various cultures. Themes from such stories appear over and over again in poems, plays, novels, and modern television and movies. The so-called Cinderella story, for example, has been a favorite of romance writers since romances were first written.

In this unit, students explore their favorite fairy tales and folk tales, write their own stories, and then analyze, in a scholarly fashion, a well-known story. My hope is that in using this material the students will learn the process of analysis through a medium that is entertaining and familiar as well as instructional.

Step One

To introduce this unit, I asked students what kinds of stories they read or had read to them as children. Many titles were brought up, and we noted that many of the stories beloved by children were enjoyed by the adults who were reading them aloud. To the fairy tale titles that came up, I added a few that I remembered particularly well from my own childhood.

Students brought up the prevalence of Disney movies made from popular fairy tales and the fact that the film *Beauty and the Beast* had recently started playing in our town. This opened our discussion of the fact that there have been many versions of this story and of other fairy tales, in both books and films. I mentioned several other versions of this particular tale, and we scanned some of the material written about fairy tales in *Spells of Enchantment: Wondrous Fairy Tales of Western Culture* (Viking, 1991). It might also be useful to assemble a few collections of fairy tales from other cultures, in case students would like to browse. The Time-Life series *The Enchanted World*, available in some public libraries, is one possible resource for international tales.

I showed students various editions of fairy tales from different publishers, including editions from Golden Book and Disney and others intended for older readers. We noted that, although the same story may vary from book to book, the general idea of the story remains the same. I referred students interested in further research to Bruno Bettelheim's *The Uses of Enchantment: The Meaning and Importance of Fairy Tales* (Random, 1989).

Step Two

Students wrote their own stories, either alone or with a partner. They wrote a first draft, which was read aloud to the class for suggestions, comments, and criticism. They completed a final draft including illustrations, covers, and so on. For this exercise I did not read or correct first drafts.

Step Three

As a class, we discussed the fact that fairy tales have been studied and interpreted in many different ways. I gave students copies of a movie review of the film *Beauty and the Beast*, in which the reviewer examines different versions of the story and the ways in which it has been treated in both books and films. (Relevant reviews of this film and of the Disney film, *Sleeping Beauty*, should still be available in back issues of newspapers and news magazines.)

Step Four

Working individually, students selected a well-known fairy tale, preferably an illustrated version, and wrote an essay of analysis. They had the option of selecting one of their favorites or choosing from one of the collections in the classroom.

Students were asked to make a careful reading of the selected work and, in their essays, to address aspects that might be relevant for their analysis. A partial list of possible questions to be addressed is shown below.

> What is the theme or main idea of the book?
> Is the theme a familiar one that has appeared elsewhere? If so, where? (Other media—television, movies, comic books, etc.—may be included.) Compare and contrast the treatments.
> What is the tone of the story?
> What kinds of language does the author use?
> What types of figurative language or literary devices appear in this story?
> How do the illustrations enhance or add to the effectiveness of the story?
> How is the conflict or problem in the story resolved?

Does the story attempt to provide the reader with a moral lesson?
Will the characters live happily ever after? If so, why?
Conclude your essay by giving your opinion on why the appeal of such stories/books has lasted so long, and why they are constantly in print.

The students were free to research additional information in the library, or to base the paper entirely on their own opinions, observations, and knowledge. The organization of the material was up to each student; however, students were asked not to merely answer the questions posed but to arrange the material in a formal essay.

Students enjoyed taking part in this in-depth look at fairy tales, and learned firsthand that not all stories read to children are strictly children's stories.

To conclude the unit, we watched and discussed the film version of Sondheim's play "Into the Woods," which synthesizes elements from well-known folk tales into an original story. This made an excellent and entertaining finale to our fairy tale project.

Sally Hellman, Las Vegas High School, Las Vegas, Nevada

3 | EMPHASIS: REAL-WORLD WRITING

ROUND-ROBIN WRITING

This writing assignment encourages students to evaluate the appropriateness of language and plot to a given audience and purpose. Because the writing task is shared, it's a good way to get off to a good start with narrative assignments and peer evaluations.

Divide the class into groups of four or five students. Explain that all groups will be writing stories geared to a specific audience and purpose: the audience is elementary school children and the purpose is an entertaining story that illustrates a familiar moral. Each student in each group is then asked to write a moral across the top of a sheet of paper. Offer suggestions ("If at first you don't succeed, try, try again"; "Beauty is only skin deep"; "He who laughs last, laughs best"; "Good things come to those who wait"; "One good deed deserves another") but encourage variety and independent selections.

Each student then begins a tale to illustrate the moral he or she selected, keeping in mind that the story should be appropriate for youngsters in elementary school. If you wish, suggest "once upon a time" beginnings.

After two or three minutes, signal that all papers are to be passed to the next student in the group. After reading the moral assigned to the paper and the tale as begun, the student continues the story, keeping purpose and audience in mind. After several minutes, the papers are passed on again. Repeat until each member of the group has contributed to each story in the group and story originators have again received their own papers. Increase the time allowed for writing with each exchange so that students can read what has been written and reflect upon the course of action. Originators of stories then conclude their stories, reinforcing the morals.

When the tales are finished, ask each group to read through its stories and choose one to be read aloud to the class. The choice should be based on the story's appropriateness to its audience and its success in conveying the moral.

As the chosen stories are shared aloud, guide the class in a critique of each one. You can judge the class's understanding of the roles of purpose and audience by the appropriateness of the story each group chooses to read and by the subsequent evaluation of the class.

Linda Frisbie, Oswego Free Academy, Oswego, New York

COLLABORATIVE STORY COMPOSITION

This writing activity gives students the valuable experience of spending two to three weeks in an environment of collaborative writing and revising. Working together, students create a story centered on a well-known character of their choice from a popular trade book series. The final illustrated copy of the students' story is sent to the author of the chosen series for commentary and return. The story eventually becomes a permanent addition to the school library, where it is sure to be a popular item.

In this activity, I guide students through the steps of the writing process while helping them focus on the necessary elements of a good story, such as setting, plot, and conclusion. I act as the scribe for the class as well, using the overhead projector to model the writing process for all drafts of the story. I distribute 3" x 5" index cards each labeled "Idea Coupon" for students to keep track of their contributions to the story line and to ensure that each student contributes at least one idea to the final version of the story.

Outlined here are the steps for conducting the activity.

1. Ask students to choose a favorite character from a trade book series. Depending on the age level, possible characters might include Marc Brown's Arthur, Judy Blume's Fudge, and Beverly Cleary's Ramona and Henry. You'll then need to assemble books, filmstrips, and videotapes for review to help students focus on story and plot development. Students will need to talk a little about typical situations and response patterns for the chosen character; this

activity works best if students know the character well.

2. Conduct a brainstorming session in which the class makes a list of ideas on novel situations for the chosen character. The most popular idea on the list is then used as the basis for full story line development in whole-group composition.

3. Give each student a 3" x 5" index card labeled "Idea Coupon." Students sign their coupons and use them during the brainstorming process to list their own contributions to the story.

4. Students talk about and plan the story as a whole group. In my classroom, I use lined overhead transparencies to copy down ideas that students volunteer as the story line evolves. Students may either copy ideas from the projection or may receive photocopies of the transparencies. I offer guidance with story elements (setting and so on) as the rough draft unfolds. Throughout the stages of revision and draft work, I use the overhead in the same manner. This helps students reflect on their work and analyze as they create.

5. In the final phase of editing, students work on copies of the final draft while the teacher works on a copy of the same draft on the overhead transparency. At this point, students locate their ideas in a copy of the final draft of the story, ideas that should correspond to items previously written on their idea coupons. The final draft should contain at least one idea from each member of the class. The teacher collects the idea coupons attached to the final draft copies.

   This step is complete when the editing is completed and each student has found (or added, subject to whole group approval) a contribution of his or her own in the final draft. Students then staple their idea coupons to their final draft copies and turn them in to the teacher.

6. The publication copy of the story is typed from the final draft. The publication copy should be prepared so that the text is distributed over as many pages as there are students in the class. I type the text at the bottoms of the pages, leaving the tops blank for illustrations. Each student then receives one page to illustrate.

   We create a book cover, a title page with an author's signature from each student, and a dedication page, all of which are then bound with the illustrated text.

7. I like to read the finished book aloud to the class, displaying the illustrations. Students also have the opportunity to check the book out to read on their own.

   Finally, we draft a letter to the series author whose character we chose to write about. We thank the author for the reading pleasure his or her books have given us and ask the author to read and comment on our own book, which, we explain, was inspired by the author's writing. We attach the letter to a photocopy of our book and mail the photocopy with a stamped, self-addressed return envelope.

My students have always received positive comments from the authors when our books are returned. Students are thrilled to read glowing comments about their own work from a familiar author. When every student in the class has had an opportunity for an overnight checkout to share the book with family and friends, the book, with the author's letter attached, is entered into the permanent collection of the school library.

I suggest that this activity be conducted early in the school year since it enhances subsequent writing projects. My students' command over the writing process improves, as do plot and story development in later writing assignments. The benefits extend into the reading curriculum as well. I find that my students can more easily identify setting, plot, and other elements of a story when they encounter them in the selections of their literature-based reading basals. This group writing activity is definitely worth a try.

June M. Hootman, Black School, Eau Claire, Wisconsin

INTRODUCING INVENTION TECHNIQUES

The idea of teaching students to use some kind of invention scheme during the prewriting process has been known for years and is widely accepted as a means of helping students generate ideas to discover what it is they want to write. An invention scheme may ask students to answer a particular set of questions, or it may encourage students to devise their own questions, but in any case the result is mental manipulation that stimulates thinking and leads the writer in new, and often increasingly interesting, directions. Of course, the invention technique will only begin to work well after the writer has had a chance to practice and become comfortable with it, and, perhaps even more important, after the writer is convinced that the technique will yield worthwhile results. As teachers, our job becomes one of introducing invention in a way to encourage its use and prove its usefulness.

In designing an assignment to introduce invention at the middle school level, the problem is particularly clear. We may see the usefulness of teaching a system like Kenneth Burke's Entad, where students explore topics in terms of Act, Scene, Agent, Agency, and Purpose, but we know that the abstract nature of these categories would make them difficult to differentiate at first. And even if we could overcome the initial confusion, there is also the possibility that students would see the invention heuristic as simply another exercise to be gotten out of the way before they could start "really writing" their papers. If we want the invention scheme to generate anything worthwhile, we must find a way to get writers involved in using it as a part of the writing process.

It is this sort of difficulty that I had in mind when I went about preparing a writing assignment to introduce the use of an invention heuristic to students of middle school age. What follows is the assignment itself and the prewriting and in-class essay of a nine-year-old responding to it.

THE WRITING ASSIGNMENT

Imagine that you have a friend who has never been to the dentist. Your friend wants to know what a trip to the dentist is like. What will you say?

Sometimes it is hard to think of all the things you want to say. Put down a short answer to each of the following questions to see if the questions help give you some ideas.

1. What does a dentist's office look like? How many rooms are there, and what do you see in each room?
2. What happens in the dentist's office? Can you name some of the different things that happen to people when they go there?
3. Who does the things you have named? What kind of people are they?
4. What tools and instruments do these people use?
5. Why do the people in the dentist's office do the things they do?

Now look at your answers and choose what you think would be most important for your friend to know. Write a one-page paper explaining to your friend what can be expected on a trip to the dentist

A RESPONSE

1. A dentist's office has a lot of rooms. Some are for only the dentist and his assistants, but most of them are for the patients. There is a waiting room, too.

   The rooms for patients are filled with apparatus. That means machines.

2. In the dentist's office, the assistant comes in and ~~tl the~~ tells you that the dentist will be in in a moment Then you wait half an hour and then the dentist comes in and drills your teeth. But he numbs them first so you won't ~~fell~~ feel anything but a buzzing.

3. The dentists and the assistants. Experienced people.

4. The dentist uses a poker with a mirror on it to see if you have any cavities. If you do he will use a big machine to drill it.

5. Because, if they don't, everybody would have rotten teeth.

In the dentist's office, you will wait half an hour when you are told you will wait a moment by the assistant. Then the dentist comes and checks your teeth. If you have a cavity, he will numb it and drill it, if you don't he won't.

At this point the student crossed out the previous four lines and started again. The essay follows:

In the dentist's office, you can wait until your turn while you read the dentist's comic books. Then he calls you in because it's your turn. You enter the room. It is a big room. It has many large machines and small tools. You might recognize one of the machines as an x-ray machine. The dentist will tell you to sit down in a big chair that has a hard-to-get-used-to light above it. He examines your teeth and x-rays them. Then, if you have any cavities, he will numb them with a medicine that he applys. Personally, I think it tastes pretty good. Then, he drills all of the plaque out of your cavity and puts a metal filling in it and lets you get down. You go back and read another comic book while your sister or brother gets his or her teeth filled.

ANALYSIS

In this assignment I tried to encourage the writers to use the invention scheme by having them write for a specific audience. While young writers might be satisfied with giving very sketchy information about the dentist to a teacher, they would want to be more thorough in describing the dentist's office to someone their own age, especially since a trip to the dentist can involve a somewhat emotional response for a lot of people. Since the invention scheme as it is presented here is directly related to the topic at hand, the student who became involved in the topic would not have much trouble accepting the questions as an aid to writing the paper. In the case of the student in the example, a review of the answers to question one seems to have led to the comforting observation that the reader-friend might "recognize one of the machines as an x-ray machine." Without the aid of the heuristic, the writer might never have thought in terms of the reader's response to the room and its contents.

In order to make the student aware of the scheme, the directions immediately above the questions mention that their purpose is to generate ideas. Then, following the questions, the writers are asked to look at their answers and to use them in choosing the information they will include in their papers. As the students refer back to their papers and choose the information they will be using, they should discover that the scheme is helping them to see their subject more thoroughly. Finally, as they write their papers, they may become aware that they have been exploring their subject and making a number of choices, a process which may contrast a good deal with their normal concept of writing. Once students have made this realization, it should be much easier for the teacher to move on to the more general form of the heuristic and help students see how it can be applied to any writing task.

Kristen M. Figg, University of Akron, Ohio. This article originally appeared in English Journal, *November 1980.*

HISTORY
IN THE MAKING
Writing for Real Audiences

At Malaga Cove Middle School, we are making history happen with our students. I call it "Project History-in-the-Making."

The California History/Social Science Framework calls for a greater use of primary source materials. We found an excellent way to involve students in meaningful writing of history. It all happened rather fortuitously when the seventeen students of the eighth-grade class of 1940 wrote a letter to the class of 1965. Subsequently the 272 students of the class of 1965 added a similar letter of their own for the class of 1990. What a wonderful opportunity for our students to get a rare glimpse into history through these primary source letters of twenty-five and fifty years ago! Now this graduating class is leaving its mark by composing a letter to the class of 2015. Future students will have a peek into seventy-five years of our history.

The lead articles from the *Los Angeles Times* and *Daily Breeze* depict a time not so long ago and yet historically important to the students, when life "seemed" less complicated. Then students are suddenly jarred by the fact that five of the seventeen 1940 grads who were Japanese Americans were in detention camps only eighteen months after the writing. It shocked our students and gave them a different perspective on the times.

After reading the letter, we issued invitations to both the 1940 and 1965 graduates, and what happened next can only be described as serendipity. Several graduates spent the day on the common ground they share with our students—the campus of Malaga Cove Middle School. They talked about their experiences as students and shared the camaraderie they had with one another. Our students interviewed them, asking about the good old days but also about the future—the future which will be the present for the graduates as of June. They related the experience as "suddenly coming upon a talking, walking time machine."

"What did you do after Malaga Cove?" was most frequently asked. "Where are you now?" "Are you satisfied?" "Do you have any regrets?" Straightforward questions answered candidly. Since each of the eighth-grade language-arts/social-studies classes is responsible for a part of the 2015 letter, many asked the returning graduates what changes they had witnessed that were the most surprising.

These wonderful people who have lived most of their lives in our communities are truly a valuable resource. Why not get people like these together with students and start a history of your school and community? It certainly worked for us.

Kathy Allen, Malaga Cove Middle School, Palos Verdes Estates, California. This article originally appeared in English Journal, *November 1990.*

LETTER WRITER OF THE WEEK

For many parents a child's first day off to kindergarten brings feelings of both joy and panic; however, soon the parents and child adjust nicely and one wonders what all the fuss was about. Seven years later comes another nerve-wracking experience for parents. Their child leaves the friendly confines of the neighborhood elementary school and enters the terrible halls of the junior high!

In my seventh-grade English class I try to ease parental fears by keeping parents informed. Beginning with the first Friday of the school year, my class sends home a weekly letter to parents informing them of what is happening in our English class as well as of important happenings within the school.

I write the first few letters on our computer. By the third week of school, students themselves have been trained in the computer lab, and our weekly letter is written by a student. As a class, we briefly brainstorm assignments and events worthy of inclusion. Each student has the opportunity to compose at least one of the final letters to parents.

After the first quarter we add another dimension to our weekly letter. Each week the class features a classmate "in the spotlight." On Monday, that student gives a brief oral autobiography. He or she must prepare an outline for the presentation, and most students bring in pictures to place on the bulletin board, which is reserved for the person "in the spotlight." Using the outline mentioned above, the letter writer then includes a paragraph in the letter about that week's featured person.

The student who writes the letter must have three people proofread it. One of these must be the person in the spotlight, to make sure the paragraph about that person is accurate. I then proofread the finished product (but do not assign a grade). After any final editing, I photocopy the letter and the letter writer distributes the copies to be taken home by the class.

Here are two sample paragraphs from letters my students have written:

Since we have been reading either biographies or autobiographies, we have been outlining our own life. Now we must get ready to be "in the spotlight." Reagan G. is going to be the first person. She is going to bring in pictures of herself, and she is orally going to give us a mini-autobiography on Monday.

On Wednesday we relaxed and read a short story called "Mr. Stang Picks Up the Pieces." It was a mystery. Now we must write our own mini-mysteries, which we will share with the class on Thursday. We will see if we are good detectives!

Obviously, there are several possible benefits from this activity. Parents appreciate knowing what's going on at school; students feel comfortable talking and writing about a familiar topic; and students enjoy the chance to use the computer, as well as the responsibility of composing letters for a real audience. In addition, I have the chance to teach or review outlining, oral communication, and letter-writing skills.

Alicia Cross, Hopkinton High School, Contoocook, New Hampshire

Is There Life after Basic Skills?

PUBLISHING A SCHOOL-WIDE ANTHOLOGY

What's in a name?" asked Shakespeare's Juliet. We might answer, "There's magic in a name," the magic of seeing your name in print. Not only your name, but your words, your thoughts, your paragraphs, your ideas. You're sharing something with people you don't even know. They're actually reading your thoughts. That's pretty heady stuff. Especially if you're a kid. Suddenly those meaningless, endless, mind-boggling worksheets on handwriting, capitalization, punctuation, sentence structure, and subject-verb agreement have purpose. Suddenly you must communicate clearly, concisely, and accurately because you want to publish in a school-wide anthology.

The production of a student-written creative writing magazine proved to our students, who were suffering from the back-to-the-three-Rs overkill, that there really is life after basic skills. Here's what to do if you want to prove the same thing to your students.

First, select a staff of six to ten students, more if you have a creative writing class-club as I have. Ours is called "Imagination Station." Students chose to take this class instead of the usual eighth-grade English class. Therefore, I must teach the regular curriculum plus creative writing and produce the magazine. As a club we have officers with a staff organized like that of a magazine: an editor-in-chief and fiction, nonfiction, poetry, and art editors.

To stimulate interest in your new project you could hold a school-wide contest to name your magazine. After entries are submitted, your staff votes on the winner which is announced as part of a publicity campaign.

It's important to inform other teachers and to solicit their help. A mimeographed note should inform teachers of the kinds of submissions you accept. We take poetry, short stories, essays, plays, one-liners, fables, short descriptions, and insights. We do not accept jokes, riddles, and cartoons. The note should also state your deadline. You will need an ample three months between deadline and distribution. Our deadline is the first day of second semester. Save yourself a hassle by not accepting submissions after the deadline. Make a plea for enthusiastic support. After all, the magazine will give purpose and direction to everyone's writing program. Suggest that teachers have poetry, short story, and essay writing units before the deadline. Also attach a sample copy of a statement explaining what plagiarism is and providing space for students to verify (with a parent's signature) that the work being submitted is original. Students should staple a signed form to each submission. They will learn what plagiarism is and you are protected from plagiarized material—you hope.

As the submissions come in, put each into the appropriate file folder: fiction, nonfiction (essays, drama, etc.), and poetry. To judge the submissions, divide them among the class with the fiction, nonfiction, and poetry editors serving as group leaders. Have each group read its submissions aloud. The students rank them with number one for superior, number two for average, and number three for poor. The editor-in-chief reviews all rankings to check for accuracy and for obvious mark-ups or mark-downs. You do the same. In making the final choices, include as many different student authors as you possibly can. One thing that will affect this is the size of your paper. Because it makes for efficient use of space, we use letter-size pages, eight and one-half by eleven inches. Our 1980 magazine was sixty pages long, accommodating over 160 entries.

You need to scrounge the best typewriter your school can afford. Call this step the "Great Balancing Act," because it is the most tedious for you. Using a fresh, black carbon ribbon, type the selected submissions as they will appear on each page. In other words, you will do the layout and create camera-ready copy at the same time. These pages are the ones that will ultimately go to the printer. Leave spaces for pictures to be hand drawn later by the art editor and staff. Make each page look balanced. If you type two or three pages daily, the task will not be burdensome. This is why you need three months. Proofread carefully.

Keep the copy neat by placing these typed pages in a separate file folder labeled "Camera-Ready Copy" where they will not be smudged. Make two photocopies of each page you type. One copy goes to a teacher-friend or administrator for further proofreading, the other to your art editor. The art staff designs the covers and title page. For camera-ready copy, they may use typing paper and black felt-tipped or ballpoint pens. Place the finished sheets in the "Camera-Ready Copy" folder.

The art staff now makes pencil drawings to fit the spaces you have left on each page. These drawings can be cut out and taped or pasted onto the photocopied pages given to the art editor. When everyone is satisfied, the drawings can be traced onto the original, camera-ready copy. Students trace lightly in pencil, then darken the penciled lines with black felt-tipped or ballpoint pens. Extra paper should be laid over the typed part of the pages to prevent smudging.

When all the camera-ready pages are in your file folder, check to see that the pages are numbered and in the right order. Has the copy been thoroughly proofread? Are cover pages satisfactory? Is the title page accurate and in place? After this final check, take the folder to different printers for price estimates. Do not overlook high school printing classes, your district printing department, or your own in-school photocopying machines. When you select a printer, collect color samples for the cover. Take these samples to your staff for them to choose. Tell the printer to use both sides of the paper. Also ask for saddle stapling so that the staples are placed in the fold in the middle of the book. Most printers will require two to four weeks to complete the printing.

After you determine the cost per copy, announce the day of distribution so students will come prepared with money. To sell ours, the English teachers had all their students write commercials. The best ones were taped on cassettes and played during the morning announcements. Not only did this involve many students, but it also provided a lesson in persuasion, composition, and speech techniques.

After distribution of the anthologies, teachers can now use student writing as a basis for teaching anything from capitalization and punctuation to irony and point-of-view. It's smart to keep a class set handy so teachers can borrow them next year to use in motivating potential contributors, especially those coming from feeder schools.

The purpose of the anthology is not to make skilled editors or grammarians out of kids. It won't. They will probably commit the same errors they always have. Yet they will see the relationship between that "dry, boring stuff" we call basic skills and the clean, beautiful discipline of standard English in their own creative work in their own creative magazine.

In short, there is life after basic skills.

Vivian Morgan Corll, Ramblewood Middle School, Coral Springs, Florida. This article originally appeared in English Journal, *December 1981.*

FAMILY LORE WRITING ASSIGNMENT

In this assignment, students are asked to write down three family stories that they have heard repeated at important family events and around the dinner table. Students are encouraged to consult family members for details. They might also ask grandparents and older relatives for tales of their growing up. Immigration stories are especially apt. If any students are unable to remember or obtain family stories, they may write stories of their own childhoods that have been told to them or that they remember.

Before students start brainstorming for stories, I tell two of my family stories. One is about the immigration of my grandmother, when her boat sank in view of Ellis Island, and the second is the story of the elopement of my mother-in-law and father-in-law, who eloped when a death in the family threatened to delay their marriage for six months. After sharing my examples I go around the class to be sure each student is focused on the assignment.

Students have several days to talk to family members and write their stories. The day the written work is due, we have a class discussion. I ask students why they think some incidents are retold and the vast majority are discarded. Students offer ideas and usually come to the conclusion that families retell stories that somehow relate to what the family values.

Each student reads one selection to the class. During this time, each time I have done this, the class has become totally silent as everyone listened. In large classes, we have been able to identify diverse cultural and ethnic values. Each student decided what was an important family value and how it was or was not reflected in the family stories.

I often lead discussions about the literal truth of the stories, leading to the conclusion that the greater truth lies in the values preserved by the recounting of the stories, not in whether Grandma had $10 or $20 in her purse when her trunk went down with the ship. As a contemporary example I talk about the heroic air battles of Prince Andrew in the Falkland Islands which, though reported by the press, did not happen. This in turn leads our discussion to the importance of myths and legends. We find different values expressed by different cultures. If we want better understanding of an historical time or a foreign people, we should study their myths. Myths and legends are simply an extension of family stories.

On back-to-school night parents commented what a positive assignment it was and how it had generated long conversations with the students. Parents also said they appreciated that the school valued something they valued.

Several students reported that they, their parents, and their grandparents had enjoyed discussing family stories together.

I return to this assignment throughout the year when I teach heroes, social values found in literature, voice, and the role of the storyteller in society.

Sarellen Shlala, Summit High School, Summit, New Jersey

| THE EXPERT EYE

When students first reach the stage of writing multi-paragraph essays, they usually need help in planning and organizing the presentation of their ideas. I designed the following writing assignment to give them flexibility in choosing a subject and also allow a similarity of format that would facilitate class instruction in the essay-writing process. In essence, students choose a person who possesses an observable skill they admire, observe the execution of the skill, write descriptions of what they observe, and then plan and carry out interviews to discover what *unobservable* thought processes, such as planning and judgment, underlie what they observed.

The instructions below constitute a three-page handout given to each student. Each step in the essay-writing process is explained. In a multistep assignment that takes almost two weeks to complete, students find this type of outline helpful. Students may confer with me as needed at any time during the process.

STUDENT HANDOUT

Did you ever admire or envy someone for his or her ability to do something expertly—swim the backstroke, create a beautiful clay pot, train a dog, or grill the perfect hamburger? The expert makes it look so easy! Perhaps experts see something during the creative process that we miss, or maybe they interpret what is seen in a special way. To learn a skill requires more than just watching and more than just following a set of directions. We must learn to see what the expert sees.

Prewriting is a two-part assignment. In the first part, you will carefully observe someone performing a skill. Then, you will interview the person observed to discover the secrets of the skill that only the expert sees.

Select: First, decide on a person you can personally observe doing the skill you admire. You must choose someone whom you will be able to interview later. The easiest type of expertise, obviously, is one which involves observable actions that you can describe. Try to find a simple skill, or choose one observable part of a complex skill. For example, acting would be a difficult skill to examine, since most of what the actor does to prepare is mental or not seen in the final production. Your mother's Thanksgiving dinner may be admirable, but you would probably want to limit yourself to describing the preparation of one dish.

Observe and Note: Closely watch the person in action. If possible, try to observe the operation more than once during this week. Keep a log of your observations. If possible, try to observe without letting the person know, since self-consciousness might affect his or her performance and give you invalid observations.

Write: At the end of the week, write a vivid description of what you have observed. Be sure to use strong verbs and precise adjectives and adverbs so that your reader can visualize the subject in action.

Reflect: Now, reflect on what you have seen and written. What you have described was really only part of the process. Such crucial elements as an expert's planning, reasons for particular actions, and the expert's own assessment of his or her effectiveness are hidden from your senses. You may have inferred plans and thoughts, but to be sure, you must ask some good questions of your subject. You must arrange an interview.

Write: Write a short paragraph explaining what you hope to learn from the interview that you could not observe directly. This should come from your reflections and help you plan the interview.

Plan: Before the interview, formulate questions—at least ten. They should be designed to get answers that reveal how your subject sees his or her work. We will formulate some sample questions in class to help you with this step, but come prepared with some ideas of what kinds of questions bring answers to complement what you observed. Keep in mind that we aren't writing full biographies in this assignment!

Interview and Record: Now conduct the interview. Be punctual for your appointment. If possible, bring a tape recorder and ask for permission to record the interview. You may take notes, if necessary, but it may be hard to take notes and listen thoughtfully. That's your main job—to *listen*. Don't limit yourself to the prepared questions. Follow through with probing questions if the response fails to tell you what you want or if something is said that you don't understand or that you want to know more about.

Analyze: After the interview, compare the subject's comments with your own observations. What did the subject's reflections on his or her actions reveal? Did these reflections confirm what you had suspected? What surprised you?

Write: Write an informative and interesting analysis of what you learned in the interview. *Do not write out a verbatim transcript of the interview*. The focus is on your subject, so avoid first-person pronouns.

Finally, add two paragraphs to the three you have already written: (1) an introductory paragraph to introduce your subject and his or her area of expertise; and (2) a final paragraph to summarize what you learned about being an expert at this skill.

Your complete paper should contain the following: introduction, observation, purpose of interview, information from interview, and conclusion.

Suggested Timetable

1. Observations made and noted. Time: 1 week.
2. Observations written in rough draft form. Time: 1 day.
3. Appointment made for interview. Time: Schedule appointment within a few days after completing observations.
4. Plan and write down the interview questions. Have these checked by the teacher before you conduct the interview.
5. Interview completed. Time: Within 1 week after observations.
6. Rough draft of interview analysis and introductory and concluding paragraphs completed. Time: 1 day.
7. Rough draft revised and edited, with feedback from a classmate. Time: Class time for 2 weeks after assignment is given.
8. Final draft prepared. Time: 2 days after class time for conferences.

This project has been very successful with my advanced eighth-grade language arts students; students learn from the writing and interviewing practice and also gain insight into what it takes to be an expert at something.

Claudia Maynard, St. Petersburg, Florida

PROS AND CONS LEAD TO WRITING

It had been a long week and Friday had finally arrived. It was almost time to go home. My students were at their learning centers. I commented to one of my students how tired I was and that I didn't feel like cooking dinner that evening. Suddenly I heard one of the other students say, "Hector was bad today, that's why you're tired." Then another student said, "Joey was in trouble in P.E. today." The third comment was about how hot the day had been. On impulse, I went to the chalkboard and wrote "Why I should not cook dinner tonight." Beneath it, I wrote the word PRO, on the left, and CON, on the right. Then I wrote the comments the children had made under the appropriate column. I explained that we were going to think of all the reasons why I *should not* cook that evening, versus the reasons why I *should* cook that evening. I explained that "pro" meant "for" and "con" meant "against"—these would be suggestions *for* and suggestions *against* cooking that evening.

The students' responses were excellent. As I copied them onto the chalkboard, I asked the students to write everything I was writing on their papers. Our excitement was interrupted by the bell, but the excitement that this activity had created within the classroom was unbelievable. I couldn't let this activity stop there. I assigned the students to write a paper using all the information that had been generated during this spontaneous activity. Already I was eager for Monday to arrive so we could continue.

The homework that students brought back on Monday was fantastic. I explained to the children that the paper they had written was a persuasive essay. I was quickly interrupted by a hand waving high in the air. "Mrs. Garza, can the class help me write a persuasive essay? I want to convince my parents to make me a birthday party." Juan was truly excited about his request.

Other students echoed his request. "Yes, yes, let's do it!" I taped a large sheet of paper to the board and wrote "Why Juan should have a birthday party" along with all of the "pros" and "cons" my students suggested.

The students had found a purpose for their writing. Of course, they didn't realize that they were also practicing important skills such as capitalization, punctuation, sequencing, listing, categorizing, higher-order thinking skills, and oral communication. Best of all, students loved what they were doing and they couldn't stop writing. They were on their way to becoming great writers and readers.

By the way, the persuasive essay worked in both instances—I didn't cook dinner that evening and Juan had a wonderful birthday party.

Maria Elena Garza, David Burnett Elementary School, San Antonio, Texas

TEACHER INTERVIEWS

Here's an interview project with something for everyone. The student interviewers have a chance to find out more than they ever wanted to know about their favorite teachers, and the interviewed teachers have a captive audience for childhood reminiscences.

Each student first writes a letter requesting an appointment with a teacher whom he or she would like to interview. The interview is to be scheduled at the teacher's convenience.

Next, the student meets with the teacher in person to confirm the time of the interview appointment and to agree on general topics to be explored in the interview. This is just a brief meeting, but it lets the student know if there are any topics that the teacher would especially like to be asked about, such as a former career in mountain climbing or a famous relative in the family, and it provides ideas for questions. Questions prepared for an interview might pertain to the teacher's childhood, family life, exciting or unusual experiences, world travels, interests and hobbies, past jobs, likes and dislikes as a teacher, views on important issues, and so on.

Once a student has prepared a list of about twenty questions, he or she practices the interview in front of the class, with a volunteer playing the role of the teacher. Students in the audience offer suggestions on how the interviewer could improve specific questions or interviewing techniques.

During the actual interview, the student takes notes to be used in writing a biographical sketch. (If an instant camera is available, the student can take a photograph at the time of the interview and include it in the finished biography. Otherwise, the teacher can be asked to provide a photograph for the completed project.) After the interview, the student prepares a rough draft of the biography by rewriting the notes in complete sentences and adding any details not recorded during the interview. I suggest that students try to make their biographies "flow" and not sound like lists of facts.

A draft of the biographical sketch is given to the teacher interviewed, not for editing or correction, but for confirmation that the information is presented accurately. The teacher jots comments, if any, on the rough draft and returns it to the student. This feedback helps students see if they have asked a question in a misleading way, failed to ask the complete question, or made an incorrect assumption.

In my class, two students interviewing a teacher jointly asked if he had any sisters but forgot to ask about brothers. Without realizing their oversight, the students stated in their draft that the teacher was an only child; they drew the conclusion that he probably got his own way often. When reviewing the draft, the teacher circled the pertinent question on the question list and the erroneous conclusion in the draft and responded in the margin, "False presumption. You never asked if I had brothers. I have two." The students also asked the teacher if he played on any school sports teams; when he said no, they concluded that he didn't participate in any school activities. The teacher wrote, "I was involved in other activities in school, but in the interview, we talked only about sports." In addition, either in initial notetaking or in rewriting notes, an "uncle" inadvertently changed to a "cousin," and a list of vacation spots visited took on an extra place-name, "Las Vegas," which, according to the interviewed teacher, "was never mentioned."

It can be valuable to discuss as a class the kinds of errors in accuracy found in students' drafts. Parallels can be drawn between the omissions and faulty deductions made by students and those made occasionally by reporters in the media.

After students correct any errors noted by the teachers interviewed, they turn their written biographies in to me for comment. When I return the papers, students correct and rewrite them in final form, attach the photographs, and make covers using construction paper and felt-tip pens. I have found that the interviewed teachers are delighted to receive these decorated biographical sketches.

Susanne Joyce, Valley High School, Sanders, Arizona

WHAT'S HOT AND WHAT'S NOT

Here's an assignment that provides a challenging way for students to develop and practice researching skills. My general instructions to students are as follows:

Visit several of your favorite hangouts: pizza parlors, ice cream shops, video arcades, ethnic restaurants, clothing stores, fast food joints, and so on. Interview customers, employees, and managers. Evaluate the service, decor, cleanliness, and the price and quality of the goods. Then decide whether you're going to rave about each place or pan it, and write reviews that tell "what's hot and what's not."

This basic idea can be adapted for use as a two- or three-day individual assignment or as an expanded research and writing project. I make it a two-week group project, in which students in groups of four do their researching, discussing, writing, and revising together.

Students first meet in their groups to decide what favorite hangouts they want to visit and what aspects they want to review. I ask students in each group to choose several establishments of the same type, for instance, several ice cream shops, pizza parlors, or clothing stores, to provide a basis of comparison.

Though everyone is to note such aspects as general cleanliness and service, students are encouraged to develop an area of group expertise—a specific area that they research and evaluate in detail. Students in one group might focus on the differences among the ice creams served in three different ice cream shops; students in another group might evaluate the effect that three different restaurant decors have on the mood and comfort of the customers.

In the first group meeting, students write down and discuss what they already know about each place. Then, sometime in the next couple of days, they take their lists of things to look for and questions to ask and visit the selected spots, either singly or en masse.

After students visit and take notes on several establishments, they meet in their groups to evaluate and write up their findings. Students could be asked either to write individual reviews, in which case they could exchange drafts for peer editing, or to work together as a group to produce one cohesive expository essay. Either way, students should include general reviews of each place as well as detailed comparisons based on their area of expertise.

After the completed writings are shared with the class, they are compiled and printed in the form of a small booklet and given to the school counselors. The counselors, in turn, give our booklets to new students in town who would like to know "what's hot and what's not."

Dee Chadwick, Flagstaff High School, Flagstaff, Arizona

MAKING THE MOST OF TV

For better or for worse, high school students tend to be hearty consumers of television fare. Use the following activity to move students out of the role of spectator and into the more active role of analyst. I give students the following instructions:

You are to watch a TV program and to write a short paper on it. Choose a program that you haven't seen before or have seen only once or twice. Let family members know that this is an *assignment* so that they try not to disturb you while you are watching. During the program, take simple notes. Who are the main actors and actresses? What happens in the episode? What is your reaction to the program?

After the program is over, write down more detailed notes, everything that you can remember. Don't plan to watch another program right after the one you are reviewing because you will need time to write down your ideas while they are fresh in your mind. In your notes you should have answers to questions such as:

- What type of show is it? (comedy, drama, detective, medical, science fiction)
- Where and when is this show taking place?
- Are the characters believable? Are they intended to be?
- Could you understand the action clearly?
- Is the show violent? If so, do you think that the violence is necessary?
- What is your prediction for the success of the series? (Consider the time period, the shows that come on before and after, the shows on at the same time on other networks, the subject, the particular audience it appeals to.) If you already know the show to be a success, explain the factors that you believe are responsible.

Take down any additional information that you may want to work into your paper, such as comments or reactions from other members of your family who watched the program, what you have read about the program in the newspaper or *TV Guide*, or comments from friends.

Then write an outline and a rough draft. One possible outline follows:

1. The title of the series, the network, the local channel, and the general idea for the series.
2. Main actors and actresses and the roles they play.
3. What happened in the episode you watched? (plot summary)
4. How well did you like the program? What did you like about it? What didn't you like about it? Will you watch it again? Why or why not?

5. What is your prediction for the success of this series? How long do you think it will last? Give at least three reasons for your prediction.

In between writing your rough draft and your final version, read your paper to one or two other students for feedback. It would also be a good idea for you to watch more than one episode of the series before you write your final version. That way you will be more familiar with the characters and setting and will be more qualified to make a judgment.

Note: Doublespace both your draft and your final version; that is, write or type on every other line to leave room for comments.

Peggy Hanson, Valley Junior High School, Grand Forks, North Dakota

A Prewriting Approach

WRITING AND EXPLORING VALUES

Many times our students are programmed to think they have nothing to write. "I don't know what to write. I don't have anything to say." Next time students agonize over the pangs of writing, smile instead of frowning. Tell them that before leaving your class they will have a topic for writing. The following questionnaire leads into an excellent prewriting session. (Remember they have to do the discovery.)

Values Questionnaire
Choose only one answer.
1. Which is the worst problem in society today?
    a. drug dealers
    b. drunk driving

      c. air pollution

      d. other _____

2. Which do you value most?

      a. world peace

      b. solutions to incurable diseases

      c. your family

      d. other _____

3. If you were President of the United States, which issues would you put at the top of your list of concerns?

      a. nuclear power

      b. environment

      c. poverty

      d. other _____

After students have time to share their answers in triads, bring them together as a class and ask for volunteers to share what happened in the group. (Tally answers if you wish.) Undoubtedly, some students will demand to speak their minds about one of the topics in the questionnaire. When this happens, I tell those students that they now have a topic for writing. The discovery comes from the students, and they feel as if they have come up with their own topics.

Sometimes we bring it a step further with role-playing. The students discover that their conversations can become supporting details for their drafts. The choice of an extensive or reflexive piece is up to the student.

Through group sharing and role-playing, students have brought their outside world to the classroom, and the classroom has helped them explore their values in daily life.

Dawn Martin, E. A. Olle Middle School, Alief, Texas

4

EMPHASIS: PEER EDITING, SELF EDITING, AND STUDENT-TEACHER INTERACTION

EVALUATION STRATEGIES

Two simple forms not only organize and expedite writing evaluation in my classes but foster feelings of self-confidence in giving—and accepting—praise and criticism. The first encourages students to look at their own writing from a new perspective; the second sets a friendly tone for peer evaluation; and both improve the quality of student-teacher writing conferences.

Writing Conference Sheet 1: Self-Evaluation

Name:

Type of writing (essay, poem, description, etc.):

I think the best sentence (or specific part) is:

The sentence (or specific part) that could use more work is:

The part that was the most difficult to write is:

I solved this problem in my writing by:

My goal for this paper was:

My editors were:

My proofreaders were:

Writing Conference Sheet 2: Reviewer's Comments

I read _____'s writing, entitled _____

It is about:

The sentence (or specific part) that I like best is:

The sentence (or specific part) that I think could use more work is:

I suggest:

_____   _____
(signature of reviewer)   (date)

Nancy Broz, William Allen III Middle School, Moorestown, New Jersey

DON'T JUST SIT THERE, TALK TO ME!
Helping Students Find Their Voices

I think this piece was a good piece. I liked it from all the other pieces.
    —Chintana

On the first day of class, I tell my sixth-grade students, "This year is going to be a time for you to think and write about what you do in this classroom. I will ask you to reflect on what you have learned from doing a particular activity. Your reflections will help both of us decide what succeeds, and what is frustrating."

Reflecting or writing about themselves and their work critically was something my students had little or no experience doing. As a result, I wasn't getting the range and depth of response I wanted. Where was their insight? Where was each individual voice telling me truths I had not heard? I believed that by encouraging my students to think and write critically about themselves, their work, and their learning, I would open the door to self-reflection and introspection. I was surprised to learn that providing opportunities for student reflection forced important issues for me as a teacher as well. Looking back at what was successful is something everyone does—particularly teachers. As I began to look back at student responses, I discovered a powerful resource for professional growth—my students!

Every school day, my students and I share our self-contained classroom; they know what works and what doesn't work, and what keeps them engaged. But I had to help them find the language they needed to reflect. Once they began to acquire that language, and as I began listening to their reflections, my own learning began. As my students learned not to be afraid of asking for what they wanted and needed in the classroom, I used their newfound voices to guide my efforts toward a more reflective and adaptive teaching environment.

> It is hard and confusing when you learn something on the board and it goes by so quickly. This is an imperfect project. I learned that math is so hard when you don't get something, and sometimes confusing.
>
> —*Jamie*

If we are going to ask our students hard questions, and we expect them to be honest, we have to be open enough to accept and act on their frank responses. Students can be insightful if given the proper encouragement. They have to know that it's okay to be truthful; that they can say what's on their minds in terms of education.

> I hated this activity because I didn't understand what we had to do . . . .
>
> —*Jenny*

Allowing students to become partners in the learning process has to include letting them ask why they have to learn about certain things, why they need to complete a project, etc.

> I would like to change the language I take because it doesn't make

sense to me. I wanted Spanish and instead I have to take Latin.
Why?

—Elizabeth

As adults, we demand to know why we have to do certain things. Don't students have the same right? Sometimes, as human beings, we don't have the answers. Luckily, life is a learning process. That's the message I try to communicate to my students.

It is a struggle for students to find language for what they inherently know about the ways they learn and engage. Students are not comfortable looking inside themselves for answers. "No one ever asked us to write about that before," each class says predictably. Students have to start somewhere, and saying "I liked it because I worked hard on it" is all they know how to say at first. True introspection involves teaching them the vocabulary, providing them with models, and practicing the vocabulary, so that everyone begins to speak the same language. I work with my students on this through teacher directed, whole-class discussions that are centered around a particular word or concept. Students examine and use their own language to define a word from their own experience. For example:

> *Quality: What does it mean?*
> More value
> Worth something
> To take pride in something
> *What makes Quality schoolwork?*
> Feeling satisfaction about it
> The product isn't boring
> Putting a lot of hard work into it
> Really try
> Not always your best work

I extend these class discussions over the course of the first two months of school so that students have a chance to practice the language of reflection and make it their own. Convincing these grumbling skeptics of the value of self-reflection, however, takes me almost the entire year.

Throughout the year, I keep insisting that students take an active role in their education. When they dig their heels in, I push and ask them more questions. "Why don't you like this? What would make it better? What have you learned?"

> What would I change and why? I would change the math we do.
> You probably know why, because I stink at math. I never can do it.

I would change it to my convenience—real easy math, not hard.
                                        —*Jamie*

Discovery (a medieval study) was a fun project to do. When we had to write a character diary, I thought it was too structured. It is a good idea (writing a diary about the same event for two separate medieval characters), but would have been better in a story.
                                        —*Alex*

The process is not easy and demands perseverance, modeling, and encouragement of my students to take greater risks. I regularly hold whole-class discussions around what makes a "good" piece of work. I ask for examples of both good and not-so-good work. I keep pushing, asking "What's the difference? Show me!"

I think this piece is better than all of the other ones I wrote. I learned that it is not how many words you write, it's what you write.
                                        —*Jamie*

I wage an ongoing battle against students' beliefs that education is a collection of correct answers, and that defining quality is my job. They are convinced that there is only one right answer for every question, particularly inside the four walls of the classroom.

If I could've practiced just a little harder for the chapter 5 math test
I could have gotten over an 85%.
                                        —*Bobby*

After a cooperative activity that first day, I ask students to take out paper and answer reflective questions. They look at me with such bewilderment, I have to resist the temptation to reach up and see if I've sprouted a second head. But because the educational system has taught them to obey the teacher, they get out their paper and begin to write.

"Why was it unsatisfying for you?"
"It was boring."
"It was sloppy."
"If the grade had been higher then I would have been satisfied."

As I have watched my students struggle to become reflective, I have learned that writing and thinking-while-writing are two different things. That first day, first week, first two months of school, my students think very little.

They respond with the first idea that occurs to them. They spend more time second-guessing what they think I want to hear than they do thinking of themselves as experts on their own learning. For example, in his first reflection, Alex wrote:

> I like this piece because it took me a long time to write it, and it turned out to be very nice and neat. I like this piece because it taught me about what I wrote and how it's supposed to be written. It's really nice making projects and learning how they work.

Alex was giving me the answers he thought I wanted to hear. By the end of the year, Alex—the thoughtful, reflective person—came shining through:

> If I had the chance to change anything about this past year, it would be that I wouldn't take it such for granted. I would try to think for my future and try to get as much education as I could. I would also care about my work more. I don't like it (my previous work) now, because the work doesn't (for me) show much effort. I wish I knew what I know now earlier.

Self-reflection is a learning process. It is not just having the language, it is about engaging in a process. Clearly, it is not mastered in one attempt—a hard lesson for students. To help them see this, I ask them to complete three introspective reflections over the course of the school year: one in late October, one in March, and one at the end of the school year. These reflections are not a graded assignment, but they are required and must be included in their final showcase portfolio. They supplement the curriculum driven reflections they complete almost daily.

For each reflection, I ask students to respond, as specifically as possible, to variations of the same questions: "What did you learn?" "What were your successes?" "What were the challenges?" "What would you change and why?" "How have you grown as a student and an individual?" "What do you need to focus on?" and "What are your goals?" I guide students through each question, and we talk about what in-depth responses might look like. We examine the language. Students offer suggestions for each question, and as we record them, each idea leads to something deeper. It's very important that students have time to listen to one another and to think out loud about their experiences. I take the time to model and discuss the reflection process with them, to tell them of its importance, and to reassure them that they can express themselves honestly and concisely. This think-aloud time is an opportunity for them to practice the process, and for me to act as mentor and coach.

After we talk about the reflection as a whole group, I give students time to look through their portfolios, and to begin developing strategies for organizing their reflective writing. I treat each of these reflections as independent work. I am very definite about deadlines (usually two weeks), and students are expected to come to me for as much or as little help as they need. The first two reflections require a lot of class discussion and individual help. The third is almost completely independent. Students have the tools they need by year's end to express their thoughts and ideas.

> I think the most important thing I learned this year was learning about Chernobyl. I am really glad that I learned about Chernobyl, because when I first got the assignment I said, "I can never do this stupid report." When I was almost done with it I was very happy. I regret what I said about it in the beginning (that I couldn't do this "stupid report").
>
> —*Jenny*

These reflections give students a point of entry for talking about their school year and their learning process. More than anything else, they are extremely persuasive indicators of individual student growth over time. When I lay the three reflections side by side, I see concrete evidence of critical thinking development; I see students struggling to express the evidence of their learning; I see students going beyond what is happening in the classroom to think about what learning means to them as individuals, as learners, and as interpreters of their own worlds. When students have the language, understand the process, and begin to reflect on their learning, they surprise themselves with what they know and what they are capable of. They discover that they really do know what they want to learn, and what they need to do to be successful. Math, Social Studies, Science, and English all come under student scrutiny.

> In math group, we had to work together doing a tangram. I didn't like my group but I had no choice but to work with them. I realized that I am not an easy person to work with. I also realized that I tend to give up quickly. When I am in that situation my brain does not function. What made it difficult was that I didn't look at all the different ways I could do it.
>
> —*Chintana*

About halfway through the school year, the conversations and practice begin to pay off. Reflections show signs of students thinking for themselves about what is valuable and necessary. Their reflections become more introspective. Instead of focusing on external causes for success or failure, my students begin to look at the process they went through that was unique to themselves.

> The most important thing I learned is not about learning, but to think about my future. I used to just come to school and learn, go home and wait until the next school day. In the meantime I was hearing people tell me to think about my future. I thought it would come to me. I have changed now. I think if I think about my future, I will be much stronger when I'll have a chance to bring it alive.
> —*Alex*

I didn't have to tell students what was good or not so good about an experience. Eleven- and twelve-year-olds are in a critical period and can see for themselves with far-reaching clarity.

> The most serious thing I did was to make my castle floor plan. I had to create a scale and measure to find the exact area of each room and building in the blue print. Studying about the Dark and Middle Ages was challenging. It was hard to understand some of the things and to find information about the people and how they lived back then.
> —*Charley*

At the end of a year of reflecting, students could diagnose what caused success or failure, what "turned them on" to learning, and what techniques they used to solve problems. This skill grew out of whole-group discussions, shared examinations and debates about work, and modeling and practice.

> I'm a very creative person, and I like to show what I can do with a piece of paper and a pen. My work was done carefully and I was very committed to it. I created a cartoony character for my book. I consider it my best piece—the text was great. I modeled the book after some kids on my street. At first I thought the book was plain and boring, so I added humor to break it up. I've become a lot better writer and editor. I've become successful because I try to be more serious (about my work), and to not make a big deal out of it.
> —*Willie*

Using language and writing as a tool to promote reflection and literacy across disciplines in my classroom has been extraordinarily powerful. I use students' reflections to show my students that they have power, that they have indeed been successful, and can and will go on being successful as they continue on their quest for knowledge.

If we don't ask the questions, and give students the language and the chance to give us their own individual answers, then we deny ourselves the opportunity to grow as professionals. We also stop short of giving students the voice and the vision they need to look at themselves as individuals and learners. Tiffany's year-end reflection is its own vision of what is possible:

> I learned how to make blue prints of a castle. I know how to do math better. I learned to keep calm and not yell. I now know a little bit of Latin, science, and cooking with groups. I learned a lot about the Medieval Ages and about the Egyptians. I learned how to use a Macintosh and an Apple computer and printer. I learned how to make games out of wood. I learned how to make a book, and a nice report. I learned how to use a mouse and a Powerbook. I learned how to swim in the deep end. I also learned that it takes time to do something hard. I learned how to write about myself and my family. I learned it takes time to be a good student.

Tammy Swales-Metzler, Thomas Jefferson Middle School, Rochester, New York. This article originally appeared in Voices from the Middle, *February 1995.*

WRITING ABOUT WRITING

Young writers are often unaware of the struggles and triumphs all writers go through as they compose. By learning how some of their peers cope with the writing process, and by examining the process they themselves use in writing, students can improve their writing and gain confidence.

I usually wait to use this activity until after students have written two or three papers and have done lots of informal writing. On the day when the final draft of a finished paper is due, I collect their work and assign an in-class paper entitled "How I Wrote This Paper." I encourage students to be as specific as possible, including all the details they can remember about working on the paper both at home and in class. I ask them to consider the following questions:

> Did you need to write in a special place?
> Did you write with the TV on? with music playing? in a quiet atmosphere?
> Did you use a particular writing utensil or special paper?
> Were there any particular circumstances or techniques that made it easier or more difficult for you to write?
> How did you get started?
> What did you do if and when you got stuck?
> Did you need an outline or notes or freewritings?
> How much did you revise?
> Did you make more than one draft?
> Did you read your work to anyone or talk about it with anyone?
> What kind of final editing and polishing did you do?
> What was the toughest part of this paper for you?
> What was the easiest part?

I allow about twenty minutes for students to write in response to these questions and then ask them to conclude by estimating how much time it took them to write and revise the paper.

Next, I put students into groups of four to read their papers aloud to each other. Once each group member has read his or her paper, I ask students to discuss the questions listed below while one member of the group takes notes. This usually takes another twenty minutes.

1. Were there any similarities among the way group members wrote?
2. Were there major differences among the way group members wrote?
3. Did anyone have an especially interesting or unusual approach to writing?
4. What kinds of circumstances did group members agree made it more difficult to write?
5. What circumstances or techniques would you recommend as making writing easier, faster, or more pleasant?

The final step is to ask each group's "secretary" to make a brief report while I take notes on the board. Usually the reports quite naturally fall into a set of prewriting, writing, revising, and editing strategies, which I organize across the board. This group sharing is often playful as well as instructive as students share their pleasures and pains with the papers they just handed in, offering anecdotes about 3 a.m. inspiration, writer's block, and the emergency trip to the store for a favorite type of ballpoint pen. We conclude by comparing the estimates of writing time, a range that may run from a low of six hours to a high of seventeen for a standard three-page paper.

By the end of this exploration of writing styles, students have some ideas on how to improve the way they write, and also have the assurance that their writing behaviors are normal. An additional bonus for me is that I find it a valuable diagnostic tool. I can see how well my message about the writing process is getting across; but more important, I learn reasons for certain students' writing problems. Problems in a paper, too, can often be explained by examining the process the student used. Knowledge about the amount and kind of work that went into the paper also makes me more understanding as I write comments and assign grades. I can compliment students on strategies they've used that have worked well, or suggest methods that might make their writing even better.

Lois M. Rosen, Flint, Michigan

Peer Response

TEACHING SPECIFIC REVISION SUGGESTIONS

I liked your story about the principal. I think you should add a little more detail and you should change the end two sentences so it will sound better.

Sound familiar? This student response to a peer's draft is all too typical of the way untrained secondary students give feedback on each other's drafts during response groups. In a national survey of 560 otherwise successful secondary teachers of writing and 715 of their students, Sarah W. Freedman (1985, *The Role of Response in Acquisition of Written Language*, Berkeley: California UP) found that many teachers grieved over the use of peer-response groups because they had difficulty getting students to respond effectively to one another's writing. Vague comments such as the one at the beginning of this piece proliferate. The students, too, complained about the writing responses, saying that their peers rarely offered substantial help with their writing. The result is that such vague comments rarely translate into effective revision, and this is unfortunate because when students receive concrete suggestions for revision, they do revise with the suggestions in mind (Nina D. Ziv, 1983, "Peer Groups in the Composition Classroom: A Case Study," Conference on College Composition and Communication, Detroit, March 17–19). For one year we studied this problem: How can we teach middle-school students to give focused and specific response to their peers during collaborative writing response groups?

FOCUSING PEER RESPONSE

For several years, in other settings with high school and college students, each of us had been using an organizational technique with our peer response groups called PQP—Praise-Question-Polish (Gloria A. Neubert and Sally J. McNelis, 1986, "Improving Writing in the Disciplines," *Educational Leadership* 43.7: 54–58). We found that this technique helps students focus on the task at hand as well as maintain a positive attitude toward the critique process.

This PQP technique requires group members (usually two to five per group) to take a turn reading their drafts aloud as the other students follow along with copies. This oral reading helps the writer to hear the piece in another voice and to independently identify possible changes. The responders then react to the piece by writing comments on the PQP form.

Praise

What is good about the writing? What should not be changed? Why is it good?

> *Example:* "Your first two reasons for voting for Bush were very convincing reasons. They made sense to me and you gave 2 or 3 examples for each reason."

Question

As a reader, what do you not understand?

> *Example:* "Why did you say you might choose Dukakis if you were older? What does age have to do with your choice?"

Polish

What specific suggestions for improvement can you make?

> *Example:* "The last reason you gave for voting for Bush was that you agreed with his international policy, but you only mentioned

Russia. Discuss his policy and at least one other country, or just say his policy toward Russia?"

Responders then share their reactions with the writer in order to initiate discussion. At the conclusion of the discussion, the PQP forms are given to the writer for use during revision.

This PQP process was introduced to our middle-school students through a "fishbowl" technique; that is, Sally and three students rehearsed and then role-played a PQP session while the remainder of the class watched and noted the process. We discussed the steps in the procedure, and then students practiced writing PQP statements.

To focus further the response of group members, we always gave students one or more focus questions which grew out of the instruction that had preceded the drafting of the piece. For example, if students were defending their choice in the last presidential election, they might be instructed to include at least three substantial reasons for their choice. Then, during peer-response groups, their focus question would be, "Has the writer included three convincing reasons for his/her voting choice?"

As we began our study of response groups with a high-average section of sixth-grade students, we found that the combination of the focus questions and PQP format did indeed keep the students on task, but as we listened to audiotapes of each group, we recognized a preponderance of vague PQP responses. We then did a more systematic analysis of the students' comments. Using transcripts of the audiotapes, we capitalized on our collaborative arrangement by first independently categorizing each student response as "vague," "general but useful," or "specific."

Vague
Comments that are full of generalities, providing little or no specific direction for revision or for transfer through praise.

> *Examples:* "Try to revise the entire second page," or "I liked this piece."

General, but Useful
Comments that are still too general but provide some direction for revision.

> *Example:* "Describe Anna better."

Specific
Comments that provide the writer specific direction for revision.

Example: "I still can't get a picture of Anna. What kind of clothes does she wear, and what do her hair and face look like?"

```
                      Types of Response

Comment/Response                  Usefulness?      Reason

1. Oh, your story is OK.

2. I thought the part about
   your brother throwing the
   spinach was funny.

3. How old was your brother
   when that happened?

4. You wrote a lot about your
   sister.  You should try not
   to.  The composition is about
   your brother, not you sister.
```

Figure 1.

We then compared our categorizations and reached consensus on those for which we had initially disagreed. Our results revealed that only 28% of our students' comments were "specific" comments, 53% were "general but useful," and 19% were "vague." Convinced that we did not want to settle for this degree of "general but useful" and "vague" comments—those which give little or no revision direction—we set out to teach students to give more specific comments.

GENERATING SPECIFIC RESPONSE

Initial instruction on generating specific comments within groups was accomplished through a series of class, small-group, and independent activities, with periodic follow-up activities.

Total Class Activity

Four sample responses given by our students in the class during a previous peer-response session were displayed on the overhead projector. (See Figure 1.) Sally led the class in a discussion of each response, asking volunteers to decide how useful each response was and to explain the evaluation. Through this inductive process, the students were led to generalize that the first response was the least useful and the last response was the most useful to the writer because useful responses are specific—that is, they give the writer a specific direction for revision—and tell why the revision is necessary. (In the case of praise, the response should tell why the specific is effective, thereby implying that it should be kept in the writing.)

Response number 1, above, does not say anything specific about the story or tell why the story was "OK," while number 4 focuses on a specific—too much attention given to the sister—and tells why—because the writing is about the brother. Responses 2 and 3 are specific—throwing spinach and age of brother—but they do not tell why being funny contributed to the story and, thus, should be kept.

Small-Group Activity

Students were then placed in small groups of three or four (pre-planned according to achievement, gender, and personality) and given the following worksheet. Students were to explain why each response was "effective" or "not effective" in light of generalizations derived from the previous class activity. (See Figure 2.)

Students worked in groups with an appointed leader who kept the discussion progressing and a recorder who wrote the agreed-upon responses. An entire-class discussion then was initiated by Sally so that consensus was reached. (See Figure 1.)

Individual Worth

The final activity to teach specific responses during peer groups required each student to select any three ineffective responses from the group activity sheet and to compose a specific response that would make each comment useful to the writer. For example, instead of writing, "Good word choice, detail, and facts," an effective responder might write, "I especially like the way you described your parents as real-life take-offs of Roseanne and John Barr. You told me how they fought over the charge cards and how John always had to do what he considered to be more than his share of the housework. He also took care of the car and yard without anyone helping him. My parents fight about these things sometimes, too, and that part of your story was really clear to me." Students received the original drafts to use in writing their comments. These revised comments were then shared and evaluated by the entire class.

Follow-up

After this initial introduction to specific responses, which took one class session, we followed up the next day by asking this question: "What are the keys to writing specific response statements for my writing-response group members? (Be specific; tell why.)" Freshly reminded of this information, students were ready for a collaborative peer response session.

Another peer-response session was used approximately three weeks later on a new piece of writing. Again, prior to the beginning of the groups, Sally began the class with a drill which required the students to analyze comments for effectiveness, rewrite less-than-effective ones, and list characteristics of effective responses. Again, comments were taken from the previous writing-response groups PQP sheet or from the audiotapes.

Drill

Choose any 3 student responses found on the worksheet on your desk. In your learning log, analyze each. Describe in specific language why you consider the response to be effective or ineffective. Then make a list of things you think are important to re member when writing a response for a writer's draft.

RESULTS OF INSTRUCTION

Recall that prior to this instruction on giving specific comments in response groups, 19% of the comments generated by students were "vague," 53% were "general but somewhat useful," and only 28% were "specific." After the instruction, which included the class activity, small-group activity, independent practice in writing specific comments, and the drill immediately prior to the peer-group session, the "specific" comments rose to 42% of the comments, "vague" comments dropped to 14%, and "general but somewhat useful" to 44%. (This change was a statistically significant one: .05 level.) After the next writing-response session, which had only a drill activity precede it, "specific" comments were up to 60%, "general but somewhat useful" down to 34%, and "vague" comments down to only 6%. (This change was also statistically significant—at the .01 level.) We derived these percentages from our independent, then collaborative analysis of audiotapes of the response groups. The percentages continued to be relatively consistent for follow-up response groups.

```
                Sample Response Group Comments

Read each of the following comments and evaluate the effectiveness
of each.

Response/Comment            This is            This is not
                            effective          effective
                            because . . .      because . . .


You need to give the
readers more information
to convince them. Why is
it better in North Carolina
than Maryland?

First sentence is too
short.  A few words are
misplaced.

I liked your story, but you
began practically every
sentence with "but" or
"so."

Try to shorten your first
sentence; it is a good topic
but too long.

Exactly why did your teacher
pick on you?

What happened when you made
smart remarks back?  What
happened after you accepted
defeat?  More specific detail
is needed to get the whole story.

Good word choice, detail, and
facts.  Sentence structure is
not too good in some places.

Your topic sentence needs work.
I don't take French and anyone
who does not wouldn't understand.

Good description of your feelings
when you lost your cat.
```

Figure 2.

Gloria A. Neubert, Towson State University, Maryland, and Sally J. McNelis, Golden Ring Middle School, Baltimore, Maryland. This article originally appeared in English Journal, *September 1990.*

RECEIVE OR RECEIVE?

Young writers are often so concerned with the spelling and mechanics of their pieces that they cannot concentrate on the real purpose of writing—to communicate a message. This activity encourages students to think about the message as they write. It reminds them that surface forms can be "cleaned up" at a later time.

The procedure is simple. Ask students to rely on their own judgment about spelling and punctuation but to underline words they are unsure how to spell and to insert circles where they are unsure about punctuation. Other problems with grammar or mechanics can be checked or marked with a question mark. What is important is for students to go on writing and thinking about what they are writing.

This simple device frees young writers to concentrate on the message. Equally important, the circles and underlinings make clear the temporary nature of a first draft: it is intentionally messy.

During revision of the first draft, ask students to use the available resources (you and other students in the room as well as dictionaries and texts) to correct or to verify the areas they have marked. Correcting their own work allows students to discover how accurate their hunches were. Since they are thinking only about problems which they themselves sensed in the first place, they are dealing with the very areas in which they are most capable of learning.

R. Kay Moss and Susan Wheliss, Wake County Public School System, Raleigh, North Carolina

| CHARACTER CLASH

"Mary," asked Kelly, "do you have my scarf?" "The one with butterflies or the paisley print?"

The excerpt above is a typical example of how middle-school students often write dialogue in their stories—they forget to indent paragraphs to indicate a change of speaker, which sometimes creates problems in understanding.

I developed the exercise I call "Character Clash" to deal with this problem. I distribute a page containing the following instructions.

As you wrote your story, did you remember that each speaker in your story inhabits his or her own paragraph? If you have forgotten this rule, you have a character clash!

Example:
    Brandonius said, "I beg of you—let me keep the money."
"No," said Dacelius, "you must perish!"

The dialogue above should be written in the form of two paragraphs, as shown below:

    Brandonius said, "I beg of you—let me keep the money."
    "No," said Dacelius, "you must perish!"

In this assignment, you will check the dialogues in your story for character clashes.

1. Count how many speaking characters there are in your story.
2. Choose a highlighter pen of a different color for each speaker.
3. With the first highlighter pen, highlight the speech of that character throughout the story. Then do the same for the other speakers.
4. Now that you have "color-coded" each characters' remarks, can you guess what you have if you see two or more colors in the same paragraph? That's right—a character clash! You will

need to revise any character clashes by starting a new paragraph whenever the speaker changes.

Teachers in my school have implemented this editing assignment in two ways. One is to use the assignment during a class narrative writing assignment. After students have completed their rough drafts, the teacher introduces the "Character Clash" exercise, using an overhead projector to provide examples. Before students color-code their own drafts, they work through a sample draft as a class.

A second possibility is to give this assignment to individual students after conference sessions. Assignment cards can be made by laminating copies of the assignment onto pieces of poster board and can be presented to students who need them. Students can be asked to color-code their rough drafts, which are then checked by the teacher to make sure the students understand the concept.

Alice M. O'Keefe, Spring, Texas

TURNING THE TABLES

I have read some articles recently that encourage teachers to submit themselves to the same writing assignments that they give their students. In an assignment that takes this one step further, I submit my own writing to student evaluation.

This assignment works best with short creative assignments, particularly with poetry. On the day that I return the first drafts of their poetry assignments, I also distribute copies of my own rough draft for a poem. I ask students to read my draft and to write suggestions to me for improving my poem. Students write their comments and suggested revisions in the margins and between the lines, just as I do with their drafts. And they are free to use the same kinds of helpful comments that I write on their papers: "This part could use more development"; "This part is a bit confusing"; "I would like to see more detail here"; "This is choppy"; "This sounds wordy"; "This doesn't add anything to the image"; and so on.

Except for a few students who are hesitant to take me at my word, the class happily plunges in to improve the spelling, punctuation, word placement, rhyme scheme, and rhythm of my draft. Lest you think that I have made it easy for them, I should add that while I sincerely try to create a poetic image, I also deliberately sprinkle through my draft some awkward phrases and transitions, a couple of creatively spelled words, some extra commas and semicolons, and several uncomfortably long lines. In this way, students are obliged to pay attention not only to straightforward errors, such as punctuation and spelling, but also to subtleties--to listen for what sounds rough and what sounds good, and to consider what might sound even better. Soon students begin to question even such subtleties as my use of symbols and irony.

On the day that I return their second drafts with my written comments, I distribute revised copies of my own poem. After giving students time to read their own papers and my revised poem, I explain why I made some of the changes they suggested and why I omitted others. This is an important step. I point out to students that since this is a creative writing assignment, they too are free to reject suggestions for change if, in their own judgment, the suggested changes impinge on their creative goals.

My ultimate aims in using this assignment were to help students develop sensitivity in writing and listening and to give them practice in revising their own writing. In addition, letting students critique my writing attempts had some fringe benefits. By the end of the school year, even those too-polite students gained courage and gave me good suggestions for revising my poem. My own writing improved under the constant scrutiny of twenty-five editors. When I finally published one of my poems in the student literary paper, imagine my students' delight upon reading "By Mrs. Robinson, with help from the 11th grade."

Linda L. Robinson, Country Day School of the Sacred Heart, Bryn Mawr, Pennsylvania

PUBLIC WRITING

Like many teachers, I try to model good writing practices for my students by writing with them. Sometimes I take things a step further and use the overhead projector to make my writing immediately and thoroughly public.

While my seventh and eighth graders begin work on a writing assignment, I begin my own draft on the overhead projector. As I write, my words are projected on the screen at the front of the room. Students see not only my revised, well-considered words, but my scratched out, ill-chosen words as well. They see me pause for long moments over a single word choice, cross out phrases and sentences, and occasionally become so disgusted with a whole paragraph that I start over again.

The first time you try this, some students may be more interested in your "performance" than in their own work. Soon, though, the novelty wears off. Then your work on the screen becomes simply a counterpoint to their own writing. Students glance up from time to time and see you facing the same kinds of problems they themselves are facing. The experience fosters a feeling of community; everyone is in the same boat.

While this method is not something I use with every writing assignment, I try to do it two or three times a semester with each class. I know it is working when students begin to raise their hands from time to time to give me unsolicited suggestions about how to improve my writing. "Mr. Z," someone will pipe up, "I like your first paragraph, but could you describe the pickup truck in more detail? I can't really see it. . . ."

Don Zancanella, Columbia, Missouri

Other NCTE Books about English Language Arts Standards

Any of the useful resources described below can be ordered from the National Council of Teachers of English by phoning 1-800-369-6283; by faxing your order to 1-217-328-9645; by emailing your order request to <kkesler@ncte.org>; or by sending your order to NCTE Order Fulfillment, 1111 W. Kenyon Road, Urbana, IL 61801-1096.

To preview these resources, visit the NCTE home page at <http://www.ncte.org>.

Standards for the English Language Arts
FROM THE NATIONAL COUNCIL OF TEACHERS OF ENGLISH AND THE INTERNATIONAL READING ASSOCIATION

What should English language arts students know and be able to do? This book—the culmination of more than three years of intense research and discussion among members of the English language arts teaching community, parents, and policymakers—answers this question by presenting standards that encompass the use of print, oral, and visual language and addresses six interrelated English language arts: reading, writing, speaking, listening, viewing, and visually representing. *Standards for the English Language Arts* starts by examining the rationale for standard setting—why NCTE and IRA believe defining standards is important and what we hope to accomplish by doing so. The book then explores the assumptions that underlie the standards, defines and elaborates each standard individually, and provides real-life classroom vignettes in which readers can glimpse standards in practice. Designed to complement state and local standards efforts, this document will help educators prepare *all* K–12 students for the literacy demands of the twenty-first century. 1996. Grades K–12. ISBN 0-8141-4676-7.

Stock No. 46767-4025

$18.00 nonmembers

$13.00 NCTE members

Standards in Practice Series

Written with the classroom teacher in mind, these resources have been developed by experienced educators to illustrate how students, teachers, parents, and schools can work together to achieve higher literacy standards. These books offer rich classroom portraits that demonstrate how enlightened thinking about teaching and learning can foster student achievement in each of the language arts—reading, writing, speaking, listening, viewing, and visually representing—through rigorous study that is driven by students' inquiry into the world around them. Keyed to grade-level ranges, these practical resources are designed as a complement to *Standards for the English Language Arts* and will support teachers and administrators as they help each student develop the English language arts skills and abilities to succeed in the coming century.

Standards in Practice, Grades K–2
by Linda K. Crafton
(ISBN 0-8141-4691-0)
Stock No. 46910-4025
$15.95 nonmembers
$11.95 NCTE members

Standards in Practice, Grades 3–5
by Martha Sierra-Perry
(ISBN 0-8141-4693-7)
Stock No. 46937-4025
$15.95 nonmembers
$11.95 NCTE members

Standards in Practice, Grades 6–8
by Jeffrey D. Wilhelm
(ISBN 0-8141-4694-5)
Stock No. 46945-4025
$15.95 nonmembers
$11.95 NCTE members

Standards in Practice, Grades 9–12
by Peter Smagorinsky
(ISBN 0-8141-4695-3)
Stock No. 46953-4025
$15.95 nonmembers
$11.95 NCTE members

Additional Titles in the Standards Consensus Series

*Teaching the Writing Process
in High School*
(ISBN 0-8141-5286-4)
Stock No. 52864-4025
$12.95 nonmembers
$9.95 NCTE members

*Teaching Literature in
High School: The Novel*
(ISBN 0-8141-5282-1)
Stock No. 52821-4025
$12.95 nonmembers
$9.95 NCTE members

*Teaching Literature in
Middle School: Fiction*
(ISBN 0-8141-5285-6)
Stock No. 52856-4025
$12.95 nonmembers
$9.95 NCTE members